A

STAIRCASE

FOR

SILENCE

A

STAIRCASE

FOR

SILENCE

Alan Ecclestone

Darton, Longman and Todd

First Published in Great Britain in 1977 by
Darton, Longman and Todd Ltd
85 Gloucester Road, London SW7 4SU
© 1977 Alan Ecclestone

ISBN 0 232 51364 3

Printed in Great Britain by
The Anchor Press Ltd and bound by
Wm. Brendon & Son Ltd, both of Tiptree, Essex

for
Martin and Brenda,
Giles and Imogen,
Jacob and Margaret.

Acknowledgements

The author and publishers are grateful to the Harvill Press for permission to quote Marjorie Villiers's translations of Péguy's writings which appear throughout this book. They are also grateful to Messrs Rupert Hart-Davis Ltd for permission to quote the poem *Kneeling* by R. S. Thomas, from *Selected Poems 1946–1968*.

Contents

The air a staircase
For silence; the sun's light
Ringing me, as though I acted
A great role. And the audience
Still; all that close throng
Of spirits waiting as I
For the message.
              Prompt me, God
But not yet. When I speak
Though it be you who speak
Through me, something is lost.
The meaning is in the waiting.

R. S. Thomas, *Kneeling.*

Introduction

1

About thirty years ago I bought, almost by chance, a slim volume recently published in English which bore the title, *Péguy and Les Cahiers de la Quinzaine.* At the time neither the name of the author, Daniel Halévy, nor his subject meant very much to me. My ignorance of the Cahiers was total. Nevertheless I read the book with mounting excitement and still do so today. Though it dealt with men and matters of that distant pre-1914 world, every word of it seemed relevant to the contemporary scene. Though it spoke to and from a religious and cultural situation vastly different from anything that I, a priest of the Church of England, then working in a down town Sheffield parish, had ever known, I found it an illuminating book, that is to say, a book which threw light upon and defined many problems and questions which I had felt, albeit confusedly, to be of supreme importance to me and my generation.

It did more than that. As I went on reflecting upon Péguy's work in the years that followed that introduction, learning to use it as I now believe it should be used, that is, as an aid to praying, I came to regard him more and more as one whose voice was desperately needed to be heard in the world today. It was not easy even so to continue learning from him. At first sight he was an awkward unprepossessing figure and his manner of writing at odds with our popular styles. It would have been foolish too, as

1

he himself said, to try to make him out to be a saint or prophet or Father of the Church. He did not fit into any preconceived notions of such people at all, and for that and other reasons it was easy despite the interest he aroused to lose sight of him altogether.

He came very near to that. In a book published at the same time as that of Halévy under the title *No Voice is Wholly Lost,* Harry Slochower described a great gallery of writers and thinkers whose words he deemed relevant to the cultural situation of mankind in the modern world, an impressive array of novelists, poets, playwrights, philosophers, and political thinkers. Among them were a great many Frenchmen: Bergson, Céline, Claudel, Rolland, Gide, Malraux, Maurras and Proust, but Péguy received no mention. [1] His voice was apparently lost completely, his work forgotten.

Among Frenchmen, it is true, his name evoked respect and irritation. He simply would not go away. Neither would the issues and problems that he had so stormily fought for. Like Hamlet's father's ghost he haunted the scene. As the problems of the inter-war years took on more terrible forms this figure of Péguy appeared to grow more demanding of respect. He was there to be questioned anew, and as Georges Bernanos said, he always answered. "A certain idea of France" that his countrymen in dire need craved to be repossessed of was felt to be embodied in him. As so many things slid towards confusion Péguy stood his ground. His passionate exaltation of Joan of Arc became a symbol of hope, and hope was the constant note of all his work. Men came to see that not only France but the world itself must recover that kind of interior life which according to Péguy's vision of her the Maid had known, and in the strength of which she faced her task upon the banks of the Loire.

'Innocente elle allait vers le plus grand des sorts.' [2] A setting out to meet whatever might assault both body and soul.

This book is not a study of Péguy as a writer for I am not com-

---

1. G. B. Shaw in the Preface to St. Joan, mentions Shakespeare, Voltaire, Schiller and Anatole France but makes no mention of Péguy when discussing writers on Joan.
2. 'In innocence she moved towards her destiny.'

petent to attempt it. It is not primarily a book about prayer of
which there are many already, though praying must enter very
deeply into it. It is an attempt to stay in Péguy's company, like
going on a walk with him, to watch how he set about living, to
listen to what he said about its problems, to reflect as fully as
possible on this observation of the man and his work, and to consider its bearing on our spirituality today. Every great man's life
illuminates our own. The longer we stay with him, the more we
learn from him, the more our own life becomes mingled with
his, and through his with a common life of self-transcending
scope. We enter through him, in so far as we learn to grow in
communion with him, a life at once more charged with human
possibilities, more exposed to conflict and contradiction, more
rich in resources. Such men are often the means by which we
become what we claim already to be – the heirs of Christ, in-
heritors of the Kingdom of God.

It cannot at any time be easy to do this. Those who knew
Péguy in the flesh found it hard to go along with him. There
were times when he seemed almost determined to shake them off.
Even sixty years later we must not suppose that it is easier now.
This man's voice can still be as abruptly disconcerting, as
searching, as exposing, as ever. For that reason we can speak of
him as a living voice, a voice that addresses us directly, a voice
that we cannot pretend not to have heard. He did not, and he
does not now, found a movement, expound a doctrine or lay
down a rule of life. He offers no systematic teaching on prayer or
politics though he has much to say of both.

We have in fact to do for ourselves anything which we
propose to learn from him. To speak of him as a living voice
means that we expect to be learning afresh from him as we persist
in going along with him. There is no finished Péguy doctrine.
Words which Peter Brown used of St Augustine come to mind
in relation to Péguy: 'The problem is no longer one of
"training" a man for a task he will later accomplish: it is one of
making him "wider", of increasing his capacity, at least, to take
in something of what he will never hope to grasp completely in
this life.' To stay with Péguy in this way is to be made sharply

aware of great demands being made on us as human beings living
in this modern world, of still greater things to come in the shaping of a new world that lies ahead, of the great expectations
which must characterise the life of christians in such a time.

The great task of which Péguy was aware and to which he
points us is nothing less than the re-creation of christian spirituality in terms as wide as the whole earth and the infinitely complex
relations of men and nations in this world-society. I see it thrown
into relief for us by the profound and moving study which Dom
David Knowles made of the Monastic Orders in England up to
the time of the Dissolution of the Monasteries. Monasticism had
represented for several centuries the most considerable medium
through which christian spirituality was nurtured and com-
municated in European society. In its devotional and intellectual
life it set the pattern of Christendom, frequently renewing the
impulse from which it drew strength and austerity of purpose.
There came nevertheless, a time of decay, and in the century
prior to 1530, not only in England but throughout Christendom,
a falling off in that purpose and a weakening of standards which
prevented it from supplying new spiritual vision and energy to
men in that rapidly changing political-economic world. 'The
Catholic religion was being reduced to its lowest terms.' The
medium, even if it had been served by the most dedicated men,
was no longer able to confront society with a spirituality commensurate with the problems of human life in the new situation.
'The bare ruined choirs' remind us not only of the rapacity of
those who fell upon the monastic world to despoil its wealth but
also of a failure on the part of what had once been the great
stimulating spiritual factor in European life to meet new
demands.

Whatever may have been the intentions, efforts, successes or
failures of the christian churches in the intervening centuries, it is
true that we now face a situation in which a still greater demand
is being made for an 'adequate' spirituality. It is not profitable to
try to compare the situation of the Dark Ages in which
Monasticism provided its answer or the Renaissance world in
which Reformation and Counter-Reformation offered their own

alternatives with our own. New and still newer features supplied every day to create a new world require us to look forward more than ever before, to travel more lightly unencumbered by our past, to be more alert to the signs of the times, and above all to be more expectant of God's help in the most unlooked for situations.

The key to such re-shaping of christian life lies, I believe, as always before in the way we set about praying, for it is here that the spiritual energy, the sense of direction, the will to adventure, the faith to endure, the love to embrace and the hope to continue are all recruited. The very tissues of the christian body of enterprise in the modern world must lack vitality and fall apart unless we can pray together with a strength greater than that of the disruptive forces which operate in this situation. We have examples enough to warn us of what happens when human societies fail to enable their members to adapt themselves to a changing world-scene. We may ask ourselves what grounds we have for supposing that our advanced societies will be able to do this in the face of the changes now going on more successfully than the 'failed' régimes of the past. There are experts in the sociological field who argue indeed that 'there is nothing in the human make-up permitting the conclusion that we can adapt ourselves, beyond certain ranges and boundaries, to the rapid and complex changes of a man-created order'. David Jenkins has asked 'What serious hope is there of bringing about the expansion in consciousness and sensibility which is demanded of human beings' in this survival situation?

It is this world-problem and its bearing on personal life which is the assignment to which Péguy pointed our attention. It is no less the situation in which his own attempted answer in terms of praying was worked out. He did in the first place what Matthew Arnold described as the work of Goethe:

> 'He took the suffering human race,
> He read each wound, each weakness clear —
> And struck his finger on the place
> And said Thou ailest here, and here.'

But he did more than that. He stood among the suffering, suffered greatly himself, and made his whole life a search for the source of healing and renewal of spirit. It is this identification of himself with a world in pain, in travail, that gives to his poetry and praying its true dimension. He was, to use Kierkegaard's expression, 'a serious man', who sought without ceasing active participation in the making of Man. He stands apart that he may enter fully into the process of finding out what it means to be fully human. Readily confessing himself a sinner, he glories in the Divine giving that crowns this humanity with infinite honour. He moves with instinctive sureness towards the points of conflict and contradiction. His conception of himself was that of a man posted to the frontier. His true greatness lay in seeing where that frontier was, seeing how it ran through the heart of Europe and from there through every continent of the world, but running also through our sense of history, of religion, of political purpose and the creativity of human culture. Péguy did not offer political prophecies. He registered accurately the tremors and tensions of the developing 20th century world, the ideological concealments which it affected and the defensive rigidities with which both Church and State endeavoured to safeguard their interests. He traced out the lines of variance which divided men from each other, from themselves and from the earth they were preparing to exploit in feverish and reckless fashion. He stayed faithful to his posting. 'All my life I have lived with suit-cases packed ready to move' said a woman to me years ago, herself a refugee from Eastern Europe. Péguy packed and repacked his bag many times in order to stay where the frontier ran.

It runs of course, so far as we are alive and ready to respond to the Spirit at work, through ourselves, so that to learn from this frontiersman we have to be ready to make our own journey into the interior. Péguy was no theoretician, content to offer analysis of the situation and to stand back. Faith meant day-to-day participation in the whole struggle that this making of Man involved. In using Péguy as a guide I have found myself seeing him defined by those questions which von Hügel asked about the conditions attending the kind of spiritual renewal of which we have spoken. 'We asked,' he said, 'how any deeper will-moving intercommunication can even be possible among men? For the mere possession of, and appeal to elementary forms of abstract thinking, which seem to be our only common material, instrument and measure of persuasion, appear never, of themselves, to move the will, or indeed, the feelings: whereas all that is endowed with such directly will-moving power appears not only as specifically concrete and as hopelessly boxed-up within the four corners of our mutually exclusive individualities, but also as vitiated, even for each several owner, by an essentially fitful and fanciful subjectivity.' He went on to speak of the kind of persuasive life that was needed to be a truly winning agency, capable of making for spiritual re-creation. He saw it needing to be large and alive enough 'to retain within its own experimental range at least some of the poignant question and conflict, as well as the peace-bringing solution and calm' that the times demanded. Péguy was such a man. Poet, craftsman, christian, layman, husband, father, a poor man and one deeply involved in the conflicts of the social-political scene, he was in thought, feeling and will a committed man. The range of his sensibility, the degree of his commitment, the vitality of his sense of communion with others, gave him an extraordinary position. He is a good guide because he neither cheated nor deceived himself in setting about his task.

Péguy was a man uniquely able to provide what George Steiner has called 'a field of prepared echoes', echoes that sound back as far as Eve herself, linger round Orléans and Chartres, and come to us compounded from the spiritual experience of the past without deadening our attention to the sounds we must hear today. To hear what he really says men have to be silent and ready to be sensitised beyond the ordinary range of our current speech. This again is one of the tasks of prayer, of the making of our ladder of silence.

It does not come easily in the modern world. Becoming absorbed in the one-dimensional current of instant speech we are in danger of losing both will and ability to attend to echoes. Still less are we ready to wait on what lies beyond them. The suggestion that we need to do so is likely to be received with incredulity or incomprehension by many people today. Does it really matter? Are we any the better off if we have ears to hear 'the notes that are/The ghostly language of the ancient earth'? More important still, what happens to the children of a Mother-tongue when no-one knows how to listen? What happens to the Word when it is arrested and regimented to the sloganising of Church and State? How free are men when their words are slaves? Each year we extend our uses of the media of communication, each year the Babel of tongues grows more stridently oppressive. Our problem is not that the trumpet now gives an uncertain sound, but that too many trumpets proclaim their certainties, too many loudspeakers claim attention and submission. Our modern Sower does not sow words that need sunlight and soil, rain and time, in which to strike root and grow, but sows pre-packaged replies. Péguy in this respect is claiming attention that leaves men free. Listening means liberation.

No easy companion then, but a man inexhaustibly rich. He knew times, particularly in regard to prayer when he came to a complete halt, when he felt quite unable to use the words of the Lord's prayer, though he could speak of it later as the very birth of praying. He allows fully for our seasons of blankness. He also knew the condition of being unchurched, which sets him alongside most people today, but as one who hungered for communion, for community of faith, and travelled far to find it. Any attempt to stay with him requires us to work hard in fashioning our own ladder of prayer, on which we must be prepared to descend as much as to climb. Of all who came forward to counsel Bunyan's Pilgrim, he is most to be likened to Mr Greatheart.

Few men have combined so profound an attachment to both classical culture and Hebrew spirituality, to the history of Europe and of France, to Catholic Christendom and its saints, to the Republic and its martyrs, to the working-class movement throughout the world and to the hope of a Socialist commonwealth, to a love of craftsmanship and a respect for the toil of both men and women, and enfolded all this in sheer delight in the life of families gathered round a table. Nothing of human importance was left out. Then there was always the unexpected turn that showed that the man was still in the making, still supple enough to be moulded more finely by unseen hands. I know of no better description of what this looks like in the flesh than Buber's picture provided in these words:

'Consider a typical peasant, as he still exists, although the social and cultural conditions for his existence seem to have disappeared; it happens that on his day off he can be seen standing there staring into the clouds, and if asked he replies, after a while, that he has been studying the weather, and you see that it is not true. At the same time he can occasionally be seen with his mouth quite unexpectedly opening – to utter a saying. Before this he had of course uttered sayings, but traditional and known ones, which were mostly humorously pessimistic utterances about "the way of things". He still utters the same kind now, but he makes, time and again, remarks of a quite different kind, such as were not heard from him earlier and unknown to tradition. And he utters them staring ahead, often only whispering as though to himself; they can barely be caught; he is uttering his own insights. He does not do this when he has experienced the contrariness of things, but for example when the ploughshare has sunk softly and deeply into the soil as though the furrow were deliberately opening to receive it, or when the cow has been quickly and easily delivered of her calf as though an invisible power were helping. That is, he utters his own insights if he has experienced the grace of things, if he has once again experienced despite all contrariness that man participates in the being of the world'.

Péguy knew both the contrariness and the grace of things. He knew also the loneliness and the togetherness of those who wrestle with God. Few can have experienced participation in the being of the world in so unprotected a fashion. Since so much of his poetry wearies even the most devoted reader I venture to suggest that it should be treated as whispering to himself and allowed to do its work as if overheard like wind or rain. He utters his own insights but they are anything but a series of private reflections, as his choice of the word *Mystère* to entitle his greatest poems makes clear. He, the poet, is seeing into the mysteries of God and is

himself caught up in the travail of mankind's redemption. Far
back in that story stood the figure of Jacob at the ford of Jabbok
over which he had sent his wives and children, his servants and
possessions. 'And Jacob was left alone.' He was left there by
choice to experience the mystery of the Other.

All this in his fashion Péguy knew. In his aloneness he drew an
even greater measure of strength from being in communion with
the great vanguard host of the saints of God. Knowing life to be
such a conversation with God and man, he gave it the silence it
called for. Furthermore he did not give way or retreat. He said
many times in his own way, 'Nevertheless, my soul, wait thou
still upon God' with a lot of emphasis on the nevertheless. In a
book on philosophy for the modern man, John Cowper Powys
made great use of the phrase 'in spite of'. He ran it up like a flag
of defiance against those things like pride and madness, insecurity
and anxiety, class-divisions and ill-will, which threaten to
destroy man's life, and defended it with great courage. But the
'nevertheless' which I see as characteristic of Charles Péguy faced
greater assaults and covered a still wider span of life. Péguy took
in his stride the paganism of Powys but went far beyond it. He
had much more to put at risk and much more to share.

What he had was christian faith, faith of a sort that broke
through the current acceptance of what that meant exactly as
Joan's had done some centuries before. It was at once catholic and
peculiar. Its catholicity rejected the tribalisms of devout catholics
and no less devout atheists. It was making towards that genuine
universality which today is being demanded of the Church in the
post-Vatican II situation, which now recognises voices outside its
traditional band and sees such things as human liberation not as
desirable products of the Gospel but as the Gospel itself. It was
peculiar in that Péguy refused to be partisan in the clerical and
anti-clerical battles which divided France and which lent their
fury and pride to Jules Combes as much as to Maurras and
Daudet. It was making beyond such things that encapsulated faith
in worn-out and spiritually in-turned forms. It was ready to pay
the price of its bid for such catholicity it dreamed of by staying
outside the communion it yearned to know. As Gustave Thibon

said of Simone Weil, Péguy was ready to stake everything, including his own decreation, upon Grace.

To stay with him as he prays means seeing all that happens in the life of a people quite simply in terms of its salvation, *le salut éternel*. The purity of that concern was achieved only by continual rejection of compromising terms. Writing of the part he played in the Dreyfus conflict, Péguy said quite simply: 'We achieved an existence full of care and preoccupation, full of mortal anguish and anxiety for the eternal salvation of our race. Deep down within us we were men of eternal salvation and our adversaries were men of temporal salvation.' Péguy's conception of faith had in it a far wider range of concern than that which the Church as he saw it was accustomed to contemplate. It was personal in the sense that his own personal life was meaningless apart from that of all human beings.

Is it important that we should be learning to pray in this way? I believe that our European church life, whether in catholic or protestant, anglican or orthodox, forms has so diminished that breadth of attentive concern for the World for which Christ died, so narrowed the vision of many devout and earnest people, so faltered in its critique of the powers of the world and indeed of its own life, that neither its words nor its witness stir men's lives to the depths. Too jealous of its privileged position, too fearful for its survival, too unimaginative to be bold, it has acquiesced to an almost self-stultifying extent in the fragmentation of human life. The wholeness of life, the life of the whole person, has been talked of but rarely envisaged as its proper concern. It was such a devotional vision that Péguy contended for, doing battle against both lay and clerical partisans, believing, as Keyserling put it 'that true spirit is never lay, for in its essence it does not belong to the natural order such as science conceives it; its prototype is and always will be that which the christian tradition calls the Holy Spirit'. Péguy likewise believed that the true spirit is never 'clerical', and fought the clerks as sturdily as Amos defended his right to prophesy.

2

In later chapters his work and its bearing on life and prayer will be considered in more detail. Here, a few biographical facts that are needed to put him in context in the life of the time may be given. Born in 1873 in Orléans, he lost early the father he never knew and was brought up by his mother and grandmother, themselves of peasant stock, who earned a living by working sixteen hours a day at mending chairs. His childhood had that serious but uncontaminated relation to the world he grew up in that gave an essential purity to his nature. By the time he entered the Sorbonne in 1894 he had developed an intense independence of mind, a rich capacity for friendship, and a burning enthusiasm for socialism nourished not from books but from his own first-hand knowledge of working-class life. He was never to lose sight of the fact that human society in all parts of the world was divided into two groups, a small number who owned or controlled great wealth and consumed a great part of the earth's resources, and a large body of people who consumed a much smaller part and remained in various degrees of poverty.

Péguy was not to become a disciple of Proudhon or Marx but to stick very closely to a Biblical note about the outcome of this division among men. The theoretical analyses of class-conflict might or might not be true, the facts of human experience were not in dispute. The possession of wealth and power did result in oppression and indifference and hardness of heart on the part of the rich, the lack of food, rest, shelter and freedom on the part of the poor did deprive them of opportunity to grow up to full human stature. The voices of Nathan, Amos, Isaiah and Micah, the voice of Jesus Himself, said plainly enough what this meant in terms of sin. It was *eternal salvation* that was at stake, and it was the ideological covering up of sin together with the acquiescence of Church and State in such things that moved Péguy to cry out. Pride nourished by such a pursuit and possession of wealth could not but put men's spiritual health in jeopardy. Jacob Burkhardt surveying the European scene during Péguy's youth was constrained to utter a warning. 'The secret mental reservation is that money-making is today easier and safer than ever. Were that menaced, the exaltation it engenders would collapse.' Péguy himself saw enough of that kind of exaltation to know that its causes could not be ignored.

Beneath such concern a hidden life slowly matured, manifesting itself from time to time in abrupt decisions and in the passionate integrity with which he fought out the battles in which he became engaged. It appeared no less significantly in the writing of his first mystery-poem on Joan of Arc which appeared in 1897. There was, it is clear, no time in his life when Joan did not occupy a great place in his spiritual growth. Again and again he returned in his heart to Orléans, the bridgehead of militant enterprise for the soul of France. What better place from which to start? In the Dreyfus Affair he was involved at once, and it was entirely in keeping with his whole life that when others were disposed to regard the battle once won as an incident closed, he should have insisted on proclaiming its continuing importance. In each battle he fought he sought out the timeless aspects of the issues raised, returned to them at ever deeper levels as he grew more perceptive, and set them more deliberately in the context of Christ's saving of the World.

Péguy's working life was occupied with the production of the *Cahiers,* the fortnightly papers in which he published his own work and that of others like Romain Rolland beginning in January 1900. They continued until 1914. In them he conducted a running commentary upon all questions of the day. Breaking with his original sponsors of the Socialist party to maintain his own independent judgement, Péguy toiled for the rest of his life to keep the *Cahiers* going. As often as not, it was his friends and subscribers who were shocked and mystified by the sudden twists and turns of the prolonged attack made upon all that Péguy judged to be a corruption of truth affecting the lives of the people. He spared no-one in his effort. 'The social revolution is moral or it is nothing.' Such a course of action cost him most of his one-time friends.

'Tant d'amis detournés de ce coeur solitaire
N'ont pas lassé l'amour ni la fidélité . . .
Tant de malendurance et de brutalité
N'ont pas laïcisé ce coeur sacramentaire.' [1]

In such words his life was summed up. He was to remain faithful
to that which lay beyond each step he took.

During the first years of the *Cahiers* he was an unbeliever, –
France was torn apart by battles about belief – so that Péguy
made no secret of his intention to attack the christian faith. In the
middle of the decade that opened the 20th century he declared
himself to be a believer, a christian. Yet as he insisted, it was no
conversion, no *volte-face,* no abandonment of one position for
another. It was the discovery at a deeper level of his own being
of what had been ripening there, of something never 'laicised'
but charged always with sacramental grace. It was in the descending of the ladder within himself that he came to acknowledge
with growing humility and joy a living relation with the Eternal
Spirit. Most significantly it kindled in him the imagination of a
poet, so that the *mystères* and the *tapisseries,* those never-
to-be-ended celebrations of christian insight, followed naturally.

The new life brought no diminution of the strain under which
he lived. Christians were not always ready to welcome him even
if they had managed to understand the man. Erstwhile friends
dropped off or mocked him. At home things were even more
hard. Péguy would not abandon his past; his civil marriage was a
true marriage, his unbaptised children were truly a family, and
though these things kept him outside the communion of the
Church he would not disavow them. So he went on as a lonely
pilgrim and the strain of that life found its way into words in a
poem presenting the Beauce countryside to Our Lady of Chartres. He made the journey there in the first place to put his own
sick children into the keeping of the great Mother, but the poem

1. 'So many friends estranged from this solitary heart
Have not worn out love and fidelity . . .
So much impatience and brute insensitiveness
Have not unhallowed this sacramental heart.'

embraces and symbolises his whole life. It embraced the great city
he had left, the fields of waving wheat, the villages he stayed in
on the way, the rumination that never ceased within, and, at last,
la flèche inimitable, the spire that caught the spirit as much as the
eye, and brought him tired and joyful into the Virgin's house. It
was a picture of something to be re-enacted inwardly many times
in Péguy's life. He was always turning a corner to face a new
stretch of the road;

> 'D'ici vers vous, ô Reine, il n'est plus que la route.
> Celle-ci nous regarde, on en a bien fait d'autres.
> Vous avez votre gloire et nous avons les nôtres.' [1]

It was one and the same road throughout, but the difficulties
multiplied and Péguy is to be trusted because he did not try to
evade them. The poetry was a combination of contradictions, of
desperation and assurance, of fear which he was not ashamed to
confess and of jubilation that he could not ignore. 'Chartres for-
ty-one kilometres? Now you have touched my weak spot.
Nothing is finer than a good flat road in the Beauce. The whole
problem of the human spirit stretches itself out along that road.
The whole problem of continuity and discontinuity'.

So by choice and necessity Péguy, this most sacramental heart,
made his way – 'One always knows the way' without the help of
the sacraments of the Church. It was a costly business. He had to
rely on prayer, to subject that prayer to the burden of every new
problem as it arose, to find out for himself how such praying
could take the strain. What he tells us of that experience in his
poetry demands detailed careful exploration. It has always the
factual quality of personal observation. It is always in movement,
lapping like waves of a river against the hard matter of day-to-
day life, always confirming what he knew to be true but allowing for no superficial contact. It offered no easy peace but in-
creased and deepened his concern for all other men. It meant
above all else a facing of the question of man's salvation or dam-

1. 'Only the road, O Queen, from us towards you.
This is our business, others we have known,
You have your proper glory, and we have our own.'

nation. The young Joan of Arc of his earliest poem cried out with horror over the word 'damnation', and the thought of the possible de-creation, the possible de-christianising of the world, remained to haunt him. He knew what it was to sweat with fear at such a prospect.

To very many today such words as salvation or damnation mean very little. They belong to a Church tradition that they themselves have abandoned or hardly known, to an age that has passed away. Only from time to time does the current of conventional life confront men with a glimpse, a suggestion, a warning of things in reverse, of a monstrous process of dehumanisation, of a hell that men like themselves could choose to let loose on the earth. It was with mankind moving into such conditions that Péguy was concerned. Such de-creation was, in his view, a threatening feature of the European scene, to be stemmed and overcome by patient and deliberate attention to the Word made flesh, to the divinising of all things in Christ's name.

It was the business of prayer to wait upon that, to enable men to become increasingly sensitive to its tasks, to open their eyes to its nature. When, in the *Mystery of the Second Virtue*, Péguy wrote of childhood, of the world 'where you once were', it was not as a matter of regret for a lost ideal state but as an acknowledgement of a reality disclosed to men, a glimpse of the primal beauty of the creation to be included in the vision of the glory of God. With equal fervour he analysed the political condition of contemporary France, turning each problem it raised into a decision for or against the Incarnate Lord. 'We held that one single injustice, one single crime, one single illegality, especially if it is officially registered and confirmed, one single injury to justice and right, especially if it is universally, legally, nationally and conveniently accepted, one single crime breaks through and is enough to break the whole social pact, one single forfeit, one single dishonour is enough for the loss of honour and to dishonour a whole nation'. Intolerable perfectionism? Péguy was no idealist unwilling to face the sins of mankind and his own included. He could be very satirical of virtuous men afraid of being tainted:

'But I who am not virtuous,
God says,
I do not cry out and I am not scandalised.'

and again,

'On the threshold of my temple, on the threshold of my night, wipe your feet and don't let's mention it again.'

But he also compels us to consider whether human life can afford to neglect the least plea of the least of these my brethren.

Péguy was no anarchist. He cherished the structural order in the fruit no less than the upspringing burst of life in the seed. He rejoiced in the work and achievements of men and women. He cared intensely for the slow hidden movements of growth in men and their institutions. His praying starts always from a faith in the redemptive act eternally at work. It goes on to sift out those things that obstruct the shaping of the answer that men are called upon to make. It pays even more attention to hope. 'Where there is hope there is religion' wrote Ernst Bloch, himself a strange Simeon-like figure expectant of new life coming-to-be, and the two men would have understood each other. Above all, men were summoned to commit themselves as Joan had done. *Il faut créer, il faut produire.* [1] Péguy did not doubt that the most obscure life shared in that creativity and could be raised to new levels of participation in it. He never ceased to cause God in his poems to exclaim with delight and even astonishment at the achievements of His children. He could not pitch higher the demand for a sense of wonder at the engagement of men with God and God with man.

Our intention then is to listen to Péguy and to watch how he prayed out his life in the modern world. There were many intensely personal painful problems to be faced. Of no tract of human experience was he entirely unaware, in most he was deeply involved and painfully scarred. He had no intention of bidding

1. 'One must work, one must be creative.'

Europe witness 'the pageant of his bleeding heart', but in the strange almost impossible poem written towards the end of his life, *La Ballade du Coeur,* he made known a little of the cost of the wisdom of the heart.

> 'Coeur plein d'un seul amour.
> Désaccordé.
> O coeur de jour en jour
> Plus hasardé.'[1]

It was characteristic too that he could not write about and from the heart without spanning all the creation and redemption of the world. It was the daily re-alignment of the heart in the direction of the Kingdom of God that mattered above all. It would be costly and frequently mistaken but he summoned men to press on. 'A great philosophy is not one that nothing can be said against; it is the one that says something. It is not the one with no holes in it; it is the one with amplitude, the one without fear, the one with citadels'. His was always the one with amplitude.

Since Péguy's death in the first months of the Great War the problems of the *modern world* over which he brooded have become more complex than he could have guessed. Horizons have widened, interdependence grown more intricate, powers more vast, and the temptation to treat the questions they raise in terms of manipulation grown more insidious still. The fixer is always in demand. Péguy knew that men needed time to deepen the vision of Christ in His world, needed silence to hear the voices that Joan had borne witness to, needed hope to attempt impossible things. He hungered himself for a simpler delight in the glimpses of beauty vouchsafed to men. He sought for a revolution that would transform the Church into being once more the Body of Christ in freedom and joy. He did not doubt that the whole business of prayer in which men would learn once

---

1. 'Heart charged with a single love
     Untuned
   O heart from day to day
     So put to risk.'

again to listen and hear the authentic Word was there to be undertaken by himself and his kind throughout the world. To that
end he set out upon his journey.

As for the Cross, 'one doesn't need an inscription to know
what it is. It is there planted in the earth at some place. And it
seems to know that the soil is the same everywhere'. Happy the
man who has trodden the good flat roads of the Beauce and seen
the spire of Chartres rise up to quicken his soul. Happy the man
who has not seen but yet has believed and found God present as
He will be. As I think of Péguy striding out on his much loved
Beauce, I think also of parts of France which he would have loved with an equal delight; the bare uplands of the Causses, the
Auvergne that nourished Teilhard, the warm lands of the South,
and a hundred old shrines like St. Guilhem le Désert and
forgotten places like La Couvertoirade, and so to the soil that has
nourished each one of us. It is then that St. Joan comes back into
mind, and for this occasion her words are those which Shaw gave
her to say at the end:

> 'O God who madest this beautiful Earth, when will it be
> ready to receive Thy Saints? How long, O Lord, how
> long?'

1. The Ladder

'Speak to the stones, and the stars answer.'
Theodore Roethke, *Unfold, unfold.*
'Stops and steps of the mind over the third stair.'
T. S. Eliot, *Ash Wednesday.*

To a traveller journeying southward across the Causse de Larzac between Le Caylar and Lodève there comes a moment when, passing through a short gorge, he sees opened out before him a great vista of countryside, an immensely steep slope down which the road twists and turns, loop after loop, till it is lost to sight in the plain below. He has come to the Pas de l'Escalette whose name, it is said, recalls the ladders once used by those ascending and descending this fearsome road.

Surprised as he may be by the scene disclosed so abruptly to him, he does not come to it wholly unprepared. He may never have visited the place before but it is not entirely unknown to him. Each of us carries within himself some traces of affinity with such a place, so real indeed at times that it is a cry of recognition that escapes us as much as one of surprise. Steps, stairways, ladders are already familiar furniture at the deepest levels of the human mind, rich with associations, with occasions of wonderment and travail, of grievous humiliation and of mystical exaltation. Poets, prophets, dreamers and seers have remarked upon them long ago and described their features in great detail together with their bearing upon the experience of the ascent or descent of this or that pilgrim, fugitive or hero of mankind.

Builders and artists have been no whit behind, setting out their stairways and stepped approaches to thrones and altars. The Sumerian Ziggurat and the New Hebridean pillars point the way

of ascent to some loftier state of being, some exaltation of the
spirit of man lifted figuratively towards the sky. 'Come up
hither' cries a voice whose command or invitation bespeaks a
means for such ascent, concealed as often as not until the words
are uttered.

The secret ladder whether pitched in Bethel, Mount Carmel,
Jabbok or Charing Cross has been perceived to be at the heart of
some of the most profound reflections upon the spiritual life,
upon the agonies, hopes and yearnings of restless souls.

> 'Driven out
> To climb that stair and eat that bitter bread.'

Men have variously found ecstasy, promise, challenge and fulfilment in setting their feet upon it. Nor can we dismiss such imagery lightly now as being no more than a quaint survival from
the past or fanciful indulgence of a traveller's whim. The underworld is not so distant from our sophisticated city-life nor the
desire to 'get high' so uncommon in our time that we can afford
to grow inattentive to our myths. Eden and Babel, Zion and
Gomorrah have much to tell us of the cultural scene in which we
live. Men must continue to 'look up' and 'beyond' and be ready
to descend. Immediate necessity and ultimate concern alert us to
the need to watch our steps. It is no easy matter, having hoisted
ourselves one rung above Despair, to face the disclosures that lie
in wait for us within and without ourselves and threaten to
seduce the soul, or to withstand the anxieties and perplexities that
attend the dialectics of existence.

The most profound and famous use of ladder-imagery in christian spirituality in the modern world is that used by St. John of
the Cross in the *Ascent of Mount Carmel* and the *Dark Night of the
Soul*. To him indeed we owe the special sense in which the ascent
of the soul to God is described as being made by 'the secret
ladder': secret 'because all the rungs and parts of it are secret,
hidden from all sense and understanding. And thus, the soul has
remained in darkness as to all the light of sense and understanding, going forth beyond all limits of nature and reason to ascend

by this Divine ladder of faith which attains and penetrates even to the heights of God', and 'ladder' for five excellent reasons which St. John expounds with infinite delight. In so tremendous a thing as the science of mystical love we need a step by step exposition, and this he proceeds to supply. Human knowledge is not sufficient to comprehend it nor human experience to describe it 'but the stammering tongue is not to be deterred'. 'A vertiginous ascent away from everything and towards God' Gerald Brenan calls it, and the adjective is justly chosen.

Even as I quote these famous words I hesitate, not because they do not point to and reveal profundities of one kind of spiritual experience − they lie far beyond anything that this book can aspire to − but for fear that they give the wrong impression, and because many people may well be inclined to cry 'hold, enough' or even 'more than enough' because this language simply doesn't help them. It may very well be that it proves, as William James suggested 'that not conceptual speech, but music rather, is the element through which we are best spoken to by mystical truth'.

We are in any case not setting out to study mystical states nor to make St. John of the Cross our guide. If his descriptions of the ladder of prayer leave many of us today non-starters we must begin elsewhere. We must be ready to find or fashion a ladder of our own. What matters most is that we should be wanting to set about it and facing our needs, that we should be troubled enough in spirit, even broken in heart, to want to grasp the roughest and lowliest rungs of such a ladder. The simpler imagery of St. François de Sales who speaks of prayer and the sacraments as the two sides of the ladder and leaves the rungs to be filled in is nearer to our purpose.

The ladder is to be made or discovered to be made, since in this making of prayer we are all tending towards the condition of poets who tell us in various ways that they were but instruments in the making of the poetry, out of the materials of our life in the world. Each day a vast amount of the experience that we have slips by unused − 'the chariest maid is prodigal enough' − and we are all self-starved or deprived by our own failure to put to good use the things available to us. Now and again the sunset touch or the chorus-ending in Euripedes breaks through and compels us to be attentive, to pay that kind of attention which is the substance of prayer.

In such moments we are unusually alive. We are touched by or caught up in or carried away with something that breaks in upon our ordinary restrained existence. We experience 'a quickness that my God hath kissed'. What is true of ourselves as persons is no less true of the Church itself. The moments of Pentecost come rarely to it and if it is, as some critics have said, 'a spiritually lifeless Church' it is because it has failed to use but a hundredth part of its resources. It too has failed to make attentive use of all those features, social, cultural, political, economic which make up the life of the world, which make clear men's interdependence on each other and could nourish if we were thus willing a spiritual interdependence that would transform man's life on the earth. Praying so conceived of is an act of participation in the movement of life itself or in Teilhardian terms in the great cosmic drive of the Spirit of God through all things. The ladder of prayer that we envisage must be fashioned out of its manifold works.

Men nevertheless need a freedom to move at their own pace as wise teachers have always known. Other men's words of counsel have to root themselves in our lives, dying like the grain of corn in the form they had to become an authentic word in our own. Words, imagery, silence, all need to be translated, and our praying must give us the opportunity and the sense of obligation to set about it. 'Through language', it has been said 'we construct . . . alternities of being', finding out through our many parts how to weave together the potentialities of a personal life. What is involved in such translation has been set out with vast scholarship for us by George Steiner in *After Babel*. 'The Kabbalah', he reminds us, 'in which the problem of Babel and of the nature of language is so insistently examined, knows of a day of redemption in which translation will no longer be necessary. All human tongues will have re-entered the translucent immediacy of the primal, lost speech shared by God and Adam'.

In the meantime, as he shows, the alternatives of translation must speak 'of worlds different enough to allow the mind space and wonder', must make a virtue not merely of necessity but of what has so often been deemed an impossibility. Too often our praying has been locked up in a single idiom, unable to share in a common fire. Within and without our proper tongues we are all required to be translators. Silence, humility, attentiveness, fidelity and imagination, all aspects of spiritual discipline, are involved in such a task. All tongues may declare the wonderful works of God but we need to hear them in our own.

What is it then that we are setting out to do? Using this figure of the staircase or ladder which has held so great a place in men's spiritual aspirations hitherto, we are to find out how best we may put together for ourselves such a framework of prayer-in-life and life-in-prayer. We are to look at Péguy's way of setting about it, not because it offers advice as to how to pray or a method of prayer but because it reveals enough of his lifetime's struggle to do just this to give us trustworthy help in our efforts to do it for ourselves. Paradoxically, this reserved and reticent man tells us more of the heights and depths of such an undertaking than a score of other men giving advice. But we have to learn to notice and ponder and question for ourselves the things he chooses to say. Prayer is so personal a thing that we cannot presume to share in any man's praying unless we have lived with him in a personal way, waited on him in silence, and followed the course of his life. So is it finally with our prayer to God. Our staircase commands no right of entry into His presence for a personal relation is not achieved like that. All that our efforts can do is to enable us to bring our selves-in-the-making to wait upon Him at the place where He will be to us 'as He will be'.

So we begin by watching how Péguy set about this work, the work of one who is translating life into prayer, learning to use every scrap of his experience, the range of which at first sight seems to many to be quite harshly limited, but which when handled in Péguy's fashion becomes inexhaustibly rich. 'I could go on writing about Joan of Arc for twenty years' he said, and this is no idle boast but a plain disclosure of the fact that in Joan's great venture of faith he saw the Infinite Love of God taking flesh so that there could not possibly be an end to the things he might learn from her. What he possessed was patient of such revelation. What he did was to use it, never doubting its infinite wealth. What we have to do is to follow through Péguy's working. Péguy's spirituality was not dependent upon the experience of mystical states or vision but laboriously apprehended from the fields of his everyday working life.

The fields are the ploughlands and the vineyards curtained by trees and etched by streams, the soil of the Beauce countryside and the soil of Lorraine. Stubble and ditches, fords and lonely cross-roads, patterns of trees and villages with their churches, all contributed to the shaping of Péguy's prayer.

> 'The earth that wakes one human heart to feeling
> Can centre both the worlds of Heaven and Hell.'

So it was neither Nature-worship nor purely aesthetic delight in natural beauty but a constantly renewed sense of the creation new issued from the hand of God that took firmer hold upon him. *La création est toute nouveau; toute enfante.* [1] It was equally a sense of a world built upon and out of this soil by men who made a garden of it richer than Eden itself, a garden whose sap rose in the veins of men and nourished the soul. And where else better than *dans cette douce France, ma plus noble création, dit Dieu, dans cette saine Lorraine; ils sont bons jardiniers?* [2] Much that Teilhard de Chardin was soon to expound in his great vision of earth's history was concentrated solidly in Péguy's poetry, and always with a sustained note of jubilation that the soil on which he stood and the men who worked it were part of a labouring process from which came the fruits of the Spirit. *Français, dit Dieu, c'est vous qui avez inventé ces beaux jardins des âmes. Je sais quelles fleurs merveilleuses croissent dans vos mystérieux jardins.* [3]

1. 'Creation wholly new, wholly childlike.'
(c.f. 'Earth's young significance' Browning.)
2. 'In this lovely France, my finest work, says God, in this wholesome Lorraine, they are good gardeners.'
3. 'Frenchmen, says God, it is you who made these good gardens of the soul. I know what marvellous blooms grow in your mystical gardens.'

'Issues from the hand of God the simple soul.' The second great
strand or rung of the ladder was the experience of childhood
though to speak of it at all as experience is misleading and invites
the comment Péguy made;

'Empty like an empty pumpkin, like an empty barrel.
That, says God, is what I think of your experience.'

He made it, as he wrote a good deal of the long poem on the
Holy Innocents, to glorify as fully as he could the unstained purity of human life which God delighted in at the outset of creation
and saw with renewed delight in the child Jesus and continues to
see in the re-enacted glory of childhood at any time. It is the
earnest of a consummation promised, a redeemed mankind.

Péguy had no Wordsworthian regrets for a vanished visionary
gleam though he deplored the blunting of sensibility, the loss of
hope and the pretentious time-wasting that made up so much of
adult life. He took seriously the need to go on learning from his
own childhood throughout his life. Descending the ladder meant
nothing less than being willing to face the child that you once
were, a mystery of humiliation inseparably bound up with hope
itself. Like Blake, Péguy revelled in the gaiety of children's
games and laughter but he went further in his respect for the
sense of robustly serious purpose of a child growing up in a home
where there was always work to be done and shared in. Who but
Péguy would have described the mission of Jesus Christ in the
picturesque terms of a child being sent to the baker to buy the
family's bread, not to stay chattering with the baker but to do the
errand and to return?

There is furthermore a decisive point where Péguy leaves a
poet like Blake behind and grasps the rungs of his ladder with a
matter-of-fact simplicity. The greater part of the imagery which
sustains his poetry derives from the relationship of father and
child; the prayer that embodies it is nourished and sustained by
daily recognition of what that relationship meant. 'A certain man
had two sons.' All that theologians had ever said of God was less
revealing than this story. None touched a man more closely than

this. No poet perhaps has dwelt more steadily on the two words
'My Son' to say what he knew of the nature of life. He would
have been quite unmoved by complaints about anthropomorphic
images. These types and patterns might have their ending
elsewhere no doubt but here and now as a man set himself to
pray he could do no better than to use to the full, (and who knew
what that fulness was?) the wonder of a relationship entrusted to
him. Like everything human it was assailed by sentimentality,
pride, insensibility and even hatred, but it remained the supreme
expression of God's dealing with him. 'My Son tells me . . .'
How else could God reveal His infinite pleasure in the exchange
of Love? Where else could a man find surer foundation for his
own prayer? As to the maleness or femaleness of the imagery
Péguy had no worries. The conversation in Heaven between the
Father and the Blessed Virgin-Mother was understandable
enough, and her concern for young children an obvious part of
the divine economy. She would know exactly what was wanted:

'Veuillez les reposer sur quatre jeunes têtes,
Vos graces de douceur et de consentement,
Et tresser pour ces fronts, reine du pur froment,
Quelques épis cueillis dans la moisson des fêtes.' [1]

and who could doubt but that she would enjoy doing it?

There were other rungs to follow. Young men dream dreams
and in these Péguy had his share. The Third Republic of France
was still new enough to be tense, unsure and violent, but it
offered still some room for hopes of decisive change. Péguy
learned his first lessons of socialist thought from the workmen he
knew in Orléans. He was never to lose that connection with the
men who worked with their hands, never to disavow the demand for a world re-made where the starvation, degradation and
oppression of poor and weak would be brought to an end. His

---

1. 'Your graces of acceptance and sweetness pour down
   On four young heads, a blessing to remain,
   And wreathe their brows, Queen of the perfect grain,
   With ears of corn, plucked from the harvest's crown.'

part in the struggle, in strikes and in socialist work, was prompt
and keen. Professing himself an atheist at the time he entered the
political battle as a holy war, outraged by the inhumanity of the
society of the day. With no less courage and clarity of purpose he
soon found himself challenging the socialist leaders themselves
for being so ready to manipulate men and organisations to secure
the victory of their aims. *Capitalistes d'hommes* he called them and
swung round to fight them, learning through bitter years that
followed how to detect the marks of privileged *castes* and *élites*
that battened on common men. Péguy did not desert his socialist
cause though he turned his back on Guesde and Jaurès. He learned to dig deeper into the understanding of political change,
learned to name and to turn into use the *mystique* of republican
faith, learned to know more of the continuity of a people's life.
The struggle was bitter and exhausting but Péguy did not doubt
that it rightly claimed his militancy. Wordsworth looked back to
a time of political hope when the bliss of being alive in such a
world was no doubt very real. Péguy much more matured by the
unending conflict looked into the present with undimmed fervour and cried out in spite of his pain, *le monde est bon, le monde est
bien, le monde est jeune, le monde est neuf, le monde est nouveau.* [1]

What may be called the cultural rungs of his spiritual ladder
were no less important. Péguy's introduction to Greek tragedy
came in his student days when he first saw *Oedipus Rex* and *Antigone* presented. Both were to stir him deeply and helped to
develop a dimension in his life where tragedy could be faced. As
always it turned to prayer at the last, to the kind of praying that
he himself saw tragically represented by the suppliant, the man or
woman whose life was reduced to waiting, waiting still upon
God but with an active undefeated hope and trust.

It was not difficult to relate this to his lifelong attention to Joan
of Arc since the Maid became the focus of all that he suffered and
hoped for. He did not pretend to be able to answer all the
questions that this juxtaposition of the christian faith and the increasingly secularised society of the *monde moderne* thrust upon

1. 'the world is good, the world is well, the world is young, the world is new, the
   world is fresh.'

him but he refused to put them aside. Péguy was asking how christians must face a society whose basic purposes and institutions were consciously directed against the pursuit of christian life in the world. How could the dechristianisation of France be checked? How could the falsification of the christian intention in both Church and State be shown up? The bridgehead of Orléans became a symbol of meaning in history and the prayer made round it a sustained attempt to convey a militant purpose to christian people. His own personal alienation from the Church added painful intensity to his cause. He hungered for a Church reborn while he attacked the clericals for their betrayal of what he regarded as the most sacred features of French history. In the alignments of the day, for and against the Church and its part in the education of the children of France he would take no part except to denounce both parties for their reduction of the real issues to be faced to a shameless struggle for power.

We shall need to look at the course of this battle in greater detail later. Péguy's critique of the France of his day was that of a hebrew prophet, steeped in the sense of the history of his people, outraged by the defection of her leaders, mourning their apostasy, and compelled to pray as one married to an unfaithful spouse. This rung of the ladder which cannot but deepen a sense of personal helplessness in the face of so great a corporate sin compelled him to search further for grounds of confidence from which he could continue to fight. It is in the depths rather than the heights that he found that place, in dereliction, in loneliness, and in a sharp sense of necessity laid upon him. All through his work there ran an emphasis on this compulsion, appearing in his poetry in the reiteration of the phrase, *par besoin de,* a need not grudgingly accepted but taken as witness to the truth of his commission. Compelled to go down to such depths he found himself faced by a need that enclosed both his own and that of mankind. He saw need as the bond between spirit and flesh, between time and eternity, between Creator and creature. The communion he took as the truth of living issued from such a need. No part of it could be even itself without the others. And the need had been met: *a l'éternité un temps, a l'esprit une chair, a Jésus une Eglise, a Dieu même une création.* [1] A man's life was enclosed in and penetrated by such interweaving of needs and their satisfaction: *à la vie l'enfance, à l'année le printemps, à la journée le matin.* [2] Péguy had no hesitation in speaking thus of God. He who created man thus needy – Your heavenly Father knoweth that you have need of all these things – did but extend into His creation the hunger of Love which He Himself knew. There is a moment in the long poem *Le Porche de la Deuxième Vertu* where the poet is staggered by seeing it in such terms,

> 'Il s'est mis dans le cas d'avoir besoin de nous.
> Quelle imprudence. Quelle confiance.
> Bien, mal placée, cela depend de nous.
> Quelle espérance, quelle opiniâtreté, quel partis-pris, quelle force incurable d'espérance.
> En nous.' [3]

and he runs on gasping out exclamations about the recklessness, the lack of prudence, the improvidence of God, yet catching himself out at length to cry out in wonder at such a Providence – He so loved the world, so loved the sinner, the lost, the stupidly strayed that He had need to go in search of them. Péguy's prayer as it finally discloses itself in his long poems where his imagination has given a unity to the vast range of personal, historical, political and cultural experience became an outpouring of amazed gratitude for what he had learned to see in the springs of his own being, in the Saints, in the earth and its history of this Divine need at work. He could not but believe that his own sense of wonder reflected in truth, however feebly, the wonder of God Himself. To pay was to be caught up in it.

How then to translate into our own usages this man's work? I

---

1. 'to eternity a time, to the spirit a flesh, to Jesus a Church, to God a creation.'
2. 'to life a childhood, to the year a springtime, to day a dawn.'
3. 'He has made himself need us.
   What indiscretion, what trustfulness.
   Good or ill-placed, that rests with us.
   What hope, what firmness, what tenacity, what indomitable hope In us.'

believe that sixty years after his death he can help us to pray
better in and for our world precisely because he compels us to
look from the outside in, to listen to what for most of us is an unfamiliar speech and to translate it for ourselves. It is not just a
matter of putting into English what was written in French.
When men listened to Jesus of Nazareth speaking it appears from
the records that they were amazed. He spoke in their language
but it was not their own but His. Much of it baffled them, some
escaped them, a little remained. The Word took flesh and dwelt
among men. So is it in lesser degrees with the Word being
spoken by poets and others all down the ages.

Péguy's language is unfamiliar because it is the speech of a man
of a man who went apart, who did so not to abandon the world
and become a recluse but to learn how to speak to it and of it at a
more responsible level than most of its common intercourse approached. It is what he speaks of that is important. He recognised
a great many of the problems which were just beginning to assail
in full force the modern man but we do not go to him for
solutions of these. It is not as a political philosopher or as a
teacher but as a poet that he is important. Writing of Mozart,
Karl Barth spoke of him as one who 'knew something about
creation in its total goodness that neither the real fathers of the
Church nor our Reformers, neither the orthodox nor Liberals,
neither the exponents of natural theology nor those heavily arm-
ed with the "Word of God", and certainly not the existentialists,
nor indeed any other great musician before or after him, either
know or can express and maintain as he did'. It is a great tribute
but it goes further. 'He had heard, and caused those who have
ears to hear, even today, what we shall not see until the end of
time – the whole context of providence.' It is not our business to
make claims for the stature of Péguy as much as to recognise that
this context of providence was his vision too. Creation as I shall
try to show later was new-minted for him in the French countryside. Man's redemption through Christ was the air he breath-
ed. God's delight in it all was the enveloping joy of the whole.
And so as a poet he worked to speak of life seen in that way.

To read it like this and to make it the groundwork of prayer is

no easy task. These rungs of the ladder today are even more
threatened than they were in his time by the devaluation of
words that goes on apace. In going apart Péguy took the risk of
speaking in ways that would fall on deaf ears or confound even
those who endeavoured to listen. The huge *Cahier* containing the
poem *Eve* with its many thousands of lines, repetitive and slow,
dismayed his most much-tried friends. Many dismissed it as mere
doggerel. With greater discernment Gide saw the point and said,
'What you call repetition is the probing of a man in prayer'.
Praying has used such a method throughout its history. It
is in no sense 'vain repetition' but the use of language to halt the
attention while it probes and explores the immensities of its
theme. *Eve* is the poem of Paradise Lost pronounced by Jesus
Himself, the Lord of Paradise Regained. How could it be
otherwise than inexhaustible, since He Himself had bidden men
gather the fragments that remained over and above to all that had
eaten?

There is a further difficulty to be faced in learning to use
Péguy for the shaping of our own ladder of prayer. There is very
Poetry on such a scale is rare. What gives it its worth for us
now is this bearing on prayer, yet the work of the poet can be
understood better and our use of it made more sustained if we see
it in workmanlike terms. Writing of Swinburne, T.S. Eliot said,
'That so little material as appears to be employed in the Triumph
of Time should release such an amazing number of words, requires what there is no reason to call anything but genius. You
could not condense the Triumph of Time. You could only leave
out. And this would destroy the poem'. This is not to say that
Péguy is diffuse in the manner of Swinburne but to recognise that
the poem he sought to write had its own proportions commensurate with its theme.

There is a further difficulty to be faced in learning to use
Péguy for the shaping of our own ladder of prayer. There is very
little in English poetry which lends itself to such use at the level
at which Péguy begins. English poetry for the most part
flourishes elsewhere, so that it is difficult to find poets to whom
the great christian doctrines of Redemption and Grace, the holy
Trinity and the Communion of the Saints, the Sacraments and
the Church are a vital part of the vision of life. Looking into the

past, no major english poet, Milton apart, wrote out of a passionate concern for christian doctrine, and Milton's theology set him apart from the mainstream of catholic faith. The most profoundly religious of english poets, William Blake, stands even further apart in naked grandeur. Mystical experience such as Wordsworth knew made little connection with the christian faith. There have been christian poets from Herbert and Crashaw to Hopkins and Eliot, not minor poets so much as poets of minorities, very conscious indeed of withdrawal from the mainstream of the cultural life of the nation.

What is missing from the great Romantic poets is something that Péguy took for granted while doing battle against everything that threatened it, that is, that the inheritance of French culture no matter what political order reigned was baptised into Christ and embodied a christian faith. Dame Helen Gardner has remarked upon a dislike or distaste for religious poetry evinced by some of the best well-known of english critics, and it may well be that certain deep roots were severed in the 16th and 17th centuries that cut off english religious sympathies from the sap and strength of catholic culture. She goes on to observe that 'much english religious poetry is a form of parody, if we use the word in its original technical sense of fitting new words to existing tunes, or the adaptation of the form and style of one work to become the vehicle of another with a different subject matter'. One may admire the skill of the adaptation while feeling that something of much greater importance is missing. Péguy's poetry shows none of the self-consciousness that marks so much english devotional verse. It springs from the same exuberant confident grasp of faith that built the cathedrals of the Ile-de-France. His poetry belonged to that countryside as much as the wayside crosses. He was no poet of conversion but a son of the house, and we who so often are the disinherited ones are not easily adaptable to it.

It is nonetheless with our own tongue and our own silence that we are now concerned in putting to authentic use what Péguy helps us to become aware of. What is needed most of all is a simple turned-towardness such as Buber spoke of as the single presupposition of prayer. Péguy did direct attention towards the threatened de-christianising of France, did indicate the sacramental assets within reach, did make clear the urgency of the task involved in the re-creation of a people. In the months before War came he was warning men of the approaching catastrophe and with a bitter fury commenting upon the power of money to destroy the ancient ties of a people's life. He was re-affirming at ever deeper levels his solidarity with that people, refusing to think of them as the politicians, the professors, the financiers and the priests appeared to do, holding fast to the conviction that they were even in their most abject poverty of spirit the people for whom Christ died. I believe that in our own praying today, faced by new problems of racial and cultural character, there must be still greater measure of turned-towardness, still more silent listening both to the voices of those in need – every kind of need – and to His voice addressed through them to others. Péguy's attitude throughout was that kind of listening:

> 'O mon Dieu j'aime à tout jamais la voix humaine,
> La voix de la partance et la voix douloureuse,
> La voix dont la prière a souvent semblé vaine
> Et qui marche quand même en la route peineuse.' [1]

Patient, plodding yet always sensitive prayer. He had no fears for the coming generation for there was no need to be despondent about french children, but they must be kept within reach of that unity of tradition and freedom which was at the heart of the christianised nation's life. To do that, men's praying must have already embraced these things at levels which could resist the corruption of a spiritless world. He saw that for men of Renan's generation it was still possible to draw spiritual vitality from deep-hidden springs but that all too soon a generation unfamiliar with a christian culture would be born.

1. 'God, I love ever the human voice,
   Voice of departure, voice of sorrow,
   Voice whose prayer often has seemed vain
   Yet plods its way along the weariest road.'

So the task of those who would pray was plainly defined. In their patient hopeful attention to God they must await the quickening Word, offering their bodies and minds to be bearers anew of that Word. Fidelity to that task was all. Prayer as wide in its grasp of human life as that was needed. A poet could help to kindle imagination but he too must make clear that waiting in silence was part of the task. Péguy would well have understood Simone Weil's word of warning that imagination could all too quickly offer to fill up the void spaces that grace had made and designed to fill in its own good time. He was in no hurry to fill up the blanks. What he had to do, and what we ourselves have to do, was to observe in detail the needs of a people, not to faint under the burden of their multiplicity but to see them as so many bench-marks of a surveyor's job in mapping out a wider territory for the Spirit to dwell in than any yet known.

There is an eloquent passage in Belloc's study of Danton which can help us to see a little more what this kind of prayer is about. It describes the great pageant of the monarchy of France and gives us a glimpse of that 'vast valley of dead men crowned' stretching from the first Merovingian to the last Bourbon, an over-romantic view no doubt of the significance of crowned heads, but conveying also a little of the true splendour with which the totality of a people's life is touched. The reckless individualism of four hundred years has gone far to destroy in the hearts of men a true sense of a people's continuity and common life, substituting for it a fevered nationalism which in its brutality and fearfulness is no more than the swollen egotism of isolated pigmies. Ever and again it must seek a reassurance of itself since it has no real inner life of its own by violent attack upon others. It must be seen to be richer, stronger, tougher than its rivals. What has been largely lost or checked in its growth is the generous fearless outgoing life of the persons who make up the common life open to villages, cities and nations of mankind. Robbed of that, men dwindle in spiritual stature, facing bleak destitution, sick unto death.

Yet too much of what praying is done in such conditions becomes little more than invoking God's help to be delivered from the ills of this self-chosen pattern of life. Our sense of need must go deeper than this. Our scrutiny of the character of the State and the Church must be more incisive. Our willingness to confess a spiritual bankruptcy must be open. Péguy spoke with approval of men who didn't cheat and was equally ready to say that he was nourished by everyone he met. Both comments must help us to fashion our prayer today. To set about making such a ladder we have need above all else for the gift of hope, to whom Péguy can help to introduce us as only a poet can, to hope who 'is only the promise of a bud that shows itself at the beginning of April'.

2. Silence

'What lies beyond man's word is eloquent of God'.
                        George Steiner, *Language and Silence.*
'The real word, the word of words, can only be sensed in the heart of
silence.'
                        Julian Green, *Diaries.*

We must learn first of all to be silent. When in 1897, Péguy
published his first long poem on Joan of Arc, the purchasers were
astonished and even annoyed to find interspersed among pages of
text a number which were entirely blank. 'It was', says Halévy,
'a unique phenomenon in the history of books'. It was not, even
so, altogether appreciated by many puzzled and derisive readers.
To Péguy himself it was clear and important. Why so many
blanks? 'To give you time to think.'
    It was more than this. It represented in the first place his own
willingness to pause even in a matter which passionately engaged
him, to cease from speaking, to give himself if need be years in
which to reflect upon what Joan did, what she meant to him,
what she could be shown to mean to the world. It was
characteristic of his life. Never slipshod or facile in his use of
words, he was essentially a man who journeyed gladly towards
the silence that lies beyond them, ever ready to acknowledge
with gratitude those moments and places, as in Chartres, where
he was able to find it.

> 'Voici le lieu du monde où tout rentre et se tait,
> Et le silence et l'ombre et la charnelle absence, Et le com-
> mencement d'éternelle présence,
> Le seul reduit où l'âme est tout ce qu'elle était.' [1]

37

A place where silence permitted the soul of a man to be itself in the presence of God. Péguy was well aware that years of effort were needed to bring a man to such quiet. He was loth to waste any time.

We need silence. We need to learn what silence is. We need the time and space which silence alone can provide to get the measure of our secret ladder, to face and not be outfaced by the multitudinous demands of life in the world today. We need to know the kind of silence that makes possible the kind of communication that Pascal hungered for which is communion, a thing not to be gained by dodging unpleasant things like Harold Skimpole nor by denouncing them as a pack of cards like Alice. The spirituality we seek must reckon with the mire and clay, the shouting and the torches, the accusations and the mockery. It needs silence to enable it to grapple with that task.

Contemplative prayer and liturgical practice have always known that this is so. Was it not when all things were silent, *dum medium silentium,* that the Word became flesh? Was not the Christ Himself silent at some moments, making known that a new beginning of things was being effected? So men, whether in the celebration of mysteries or in acts of prayer needed silence to make sense of the words they used, to make room for the unspoken. 'Silence', wrote Pierre Charles, 'is always more eloquent than speech, because it is far deeper and more complete'. Silence alone can provide for both the extremities of our need and the operation of God's grace, permit the insufficiencies of our attention to be checked and erase the blundering grossness of our insensitive observations. Yet we are far from honouring this necessity in the conduct of our lives.

There is in Kierkegaard's essay *For Self-Examination* an insistence upon the need for silence, couched in the form of a physician's advice when called upon to prescribe for the sickness of the world: 'What dost thou think must be done? I should

---

1. 'Look at the piece of earth, all gathered and all quiet,
   Where silence, shadow, and the ghostly reign,
   Where the eternal presence comes again,
   And soul finds that retreat where it is itself once more.'

answer, "the first, the unconditional condition of doing anything, and therefore the first thing to be done is, procure silence, introduce silence; God's Word cannot be heard, and if, served by noisy expedients, it is to be shouted out so clamorously so as to be heard in the midst of the din, it is no longer God's Word. Procure silence".'

Yet, as he went on to say to men living in a much quieter world than our own, the silence he sought was not merely a refraining from words nor was it something to be introduced into a house 'like hanging curtains'. He went on to describe it in the homeliest personal terms, speaking of it as the way in which a woman engaged in creating a home was present in her house. It was unspectacular but pervasive, deliberate but self-effacing, sustained but flexible in its powers of adaptation. Such silence was, he suggested, 'like the note, the ground note, which is not made conspicuous; it is called the ground note just because it is underlying'. Something quite fundamental to human life depended upon it, something manifest in the earliest and possibly the most influential speechless relationship of a mother and child, something capable of entering into all other relations within the home and of unifying the life of the family in it. 'Silence introduced into the house is the homeliness of eternity.'

Kierkegaard's imagery is most relevant since it sees silence as the condition for enabling a home with all its connotations of growth and unity, stimulus and forgiveness, mutuality of love and independence of judgment to be realised as fully as possible. Silence is to make possible both our true conversation with each other and, as the Taizé *Rule* observes, 'our conversation with Jesus Christ'. It is the pre-requisite of that ordering of a man's mind which may allow him to be alert rather than apathetic, serene rather than fretful, open-minded rather than fearful or defensive. It has nothing in common with a tight-lippedness nor with the cultivation of indifference.

It is upon such a ground note that so diverse a pair as Péguy and Kierkegaard come together for homeliness is the characteristic of all that Péguy thought and said of the Godhead and God's dealings with mankind, giving a central place to the woman's part in the relationship. It held together in his imaginative grasp all women down the ages, from the first Eve to the Blessed Virgin herself. It linked together Antigone and Joan and all women in their sorrows. It rejoiced at the mother bending over her sleeping child. It marvelled at the silence of the Pietà. It watched the woman tidying up the house, endlessly washing, cleaning, putting back in place those things that life disordered and soiled. It is Jesus who speaks:

> 'Et moi je vous salue, ô reine de décence.
> Vous rangez le fumier dans le fond du jardin.
> Vous balayez le seuil et le premier gradin.
> Et vous vous avancez, merveille d'innocence.' [1]

How long and laborious a job it was to make such a home and to keep it so Péguy understood deeply. No poet addressed himself to the patient observation of the work of women with greater intensity, none more closely related it to the task of God Himself who in his fatherly heart sought to draw his children home once again, into the home at night where they might sleep in peace.

> 'Enter my night as into my house . . .
>   then must it be that my Paradise
> Will be nothing but a great clear night which will fall on
>   the sins of the world.'

Night, that last created glory, would shroud at last in silence the sons and daughters of the house. The silence that must invest each rung of the ladder of our prayer belongs of right to these basic conditions of human life. Its necessity is to be learned there.

We need furthermore to be silent in order to listen. It is most unlikely that men who have grown too impatient with each other to listen to them will attach importance to listening to God

1. 'And I myself salute you, Queen of dignity,
   Who set the dunghill at the garden end,
   Who scour the threshold and the steps
   And make your way, a miracle of purity.'

or meaning to the phrase. The loudspeaker threatens to destroy
the silent area between man and man which Buber has taught us
to see as of infinite value in spiritual growth. The devaluation of
the word which has so blatantly signalised our times follows hard
upon the banishment of silence from our social life. It has been
said with justice that it is not so much the gift of tongues that we
now need as the gift of ears, not so much the proclamation of our
beliefs as the willingness to listen to the ways in which we
ourselves are being addressed, not so much the assertion of our
knowledge but the silent admission that we are ready to learn.
We have need to take seriously the counsel of King Lear; 'look
with thine ears', and to ponder no less on the line from the
Sonnets: 'To hear with eyes belongs to love's fine wit'. All our
senses are the better for being given more silent room.

To return to the Bible is to be reminded of silence as the
precondition of right relationship with God. We have always the
need to hear those questions which the Biblical writers so curtly
pose: 'Where art thou? Who told thee that thou wast naked?
What hast thou done? Where is thy brother? What doest thou
here? What does God require of thee?' – since it is these that
define and re-order the scope of man's life. Yet we have been
strangely profligate with our talking about God and to Him,
forgetting the censure of Jesus of those who supposed that their
much talking earned them the right to be heard, and meriting the
gibe of yesterday upon 'poor talkative Christianity'. Not without
relief have a great many people now found themselves beyond
reach of that institutionalised voice. 'The clerical gentleman's
voice was of a depth to claim for it the profoundest that can be
thought or uttered; and Nesta's tender youth had taken so strong
an impression of sacredness from what Fenellan called "his chafer
tones" that her looks were often given him in gratitude for the
mere sound'. Today at least the mere sound is less likely to be
welcomed but in failing to help men and women to use silence
well the Christian Church has added to rather than lightened the
burden of lostness, of isolation, of meaninglessness, felt by so
many. Its recourse to silence has been too intermittent to make it
a supremely important weapon to men battling for their lives.

Men need at all times a solvent of those devices and rigid forms which are imposed upon life, and silence is such a solvent. 'There is a kind of silence in which the hard thick shell which normally covers and protects us, the thick shell of fiction and prejudice and ready-made phrases which separate man from man, begins to crack and open'. The silence that liberates is among the great needs of our time.

'The character of the Christian is communion.' From that saying of Péguy we must not depart. Here we must treat silence as a thing that helps to make possible the achievement of communion. It has been said that in learning a language it is as important to learn its silences as to learn its words. Today certainly we are compelled to recognise the existence and importance of non-verbal languages which describe the universe and functions within it in terms that lie beyond words. In Heidegger's comment on speech it is the communion aspect that is the test of utterance. 'Keeping silent is another essential possibility of discourse, and it has the same existential foundation. In talking with one another, the person who keeps silent can "make one understand" and he can do so more authentically than the person who is never short of words. Speaking at length about something does not offer the slightest guarantee that thereby understanding is advanced. On the contrary, talking extensively about something covers it up and brings what is understood to a sham clarity, the un-intelligibility of the trivial'. In East and West alike, traditions of meditation and contemplation have taught men to distrust the power of the word which takes prisoner the user of it and to seek rather the freedom which silence affords. Much prayer has wilted and died for lack of silence to enable it to be prayer at all. Prayer without silence becomes a drooling, destructive of the communion sought for, no matter how pious the language it uses.

Language without silence is just gossip; gossipping with God is not prayer. In our own day there has been no better warning about the outcome of the absence of silence from our lives, and the consequent abandonment of the spirit to idle talk, than D.H. Lawrence's comment upon certain novels. Substitute the word 'prayer' for 'novel' in this passage: 'But the novel, like gossip, can also excite spurious sympathies and recoils, mechanical and deadening, to the psyche. The novel can glorify the most corrupt feelings, so long as they are conventionally "pure". Then, the novel, like gossip, becomes at last vicious, and like gossip, all the more vicious because it is always ostensibly on the side of the angels. Mrs Bolton's gossip was always on the side of the angels. "And he was such a bad fellow, and she was such a nice woman" '.

In such degeneration we come to grips with the essential part that silence must play in our effort to pray in truth. In Mark Rutherford's *Autobiography* there is a terrible description of the 'long prayer' with which the preacher in the services he was compelled to attend began his discourse, a performance which he could not but liken to speeches made in the House of Commons in reply to the speech from the throne. Too self-assertive in his office the preacher destroyed the right relationships that praying endeavours to make possible. 'To come maundering into His presence when we have nothing particular to say is an insult upon which we should never presume if we had a petition to offer to any earthly personage. We should not venture to take up his time with commonplaces and platitudes; but our minister seemed to consider that the Almighty, who had the universe to govern, had more leisure at His command than the idlest lounger at a club'.

It is at this point that Péguy can help us most profoundly. The silence of which we speak has no more significant description than that which he gave it in a *cahier* of 1905 under the title of *Les Suppliantes Parallèles*. We catch something of a glimpse of his own secret ladder, of 'what God had wanted to say to him' using Newman's phrase, and Péguy's own pondering on it, in the preface he wrote to a poem by Porché on the massacre of Russian workers in St. Petersburg early that year. To appreciate what Péguy wrote we need to keep in mind an observation made by Steiner on the ability of great poets to grasp the continuing life of a word far beyond its contemporary uses. 'Shakespeare at times seems to "hear" inside a word or phrase the history of its future echoes'. In due course the sensitive listening ear picks up a word that has literally gone ahead of us. What Péguy's ear laid hold of came to him across two millennia of human history, so that seeing Greek tragedy played at the *Théâtre Français* quickened in him the recognition of the significance of the suppliant. Thereafter it grew in him to become not only the key to his understanding of the nature of prayer but to epitomise his own characteristic position.

As a suppliant then he appears before us. 'It is the poet's function', he wrote 'to seize in a word, to gather in a word, the whole reality of an event, the essential reality of a tale, in a single movement, an individual or collective gesture'. Péguy saw the suppliant as an archetypal figure. Whether as man, woman or a people the suppliant appeared as a representative figure on who was laid the chastisement of the gods knit to them by the bond of the fearful burden to be borne. He was to be seen not as one pleading for some petition to be granted but rather as presenting himself as witness to the cause or contention which must, if God be God, be considered.

Only silence could be adequately expressive of the enormity of the demand. Only silence could establish a channel of communication profound enough for the occasion. The God beyond God, beyond all Gods, the God of the Book of Job, is confronted by a bowed figure whose speech dies away but whose case remains. The suppliant is there to be seen rather than heard. 'We speak with Him only when speech dies within us.' The gods of classical drama looked on and waited. The huge stage of silence, wide as the earth itself, presented an issue which touched things both human and divine. When the words of an Antigone or a Job were ended, when silence alone measured out the human condition, the suppliant left the matter at issue to the Other to do what He willed about it. Stripped of all resources, he himself could act only as a dog might do, refusing to be driven away, but being most human in making the conscious choice of staying and remaining silent. It would be a tampering with the situation and with the relationship which such supplication presumes to put into words, supposing that such could be done, what God knows to be the case. In bitter extremity words might be wrung from

such a man but they too made way for silence. In that the
suppliant waited for divine recognition of his case.

There are other aspects of prayer, on all of which Péguy had
much to say, recognising as he did that silence was needed also to
permit the recalling of what had taken place already in our lives,
a recalling not simply of those things welcomed and gladly
received but also of those more difficult matters which a man
might endeavour to thrust away or from which he would hide
his eyes. Prayer is concerned with making meaningful all that has
passed through his experience. It is concerned to find out,
perhaps to hear for the first time long after an event has passed,
what was said to a man and became either then or later a decisive
point in his life. True thankfulness to God can know no deeper
content than a growing recognition of what being thus redeemed
amounts to, what His word has in fact been making of us. 'So
foolish was I and ignorant', he exclaims with the Psalmist as the
silence thus spent reveals something more of what has been done
by Grace, something even of that essential imperfection hidden in
the depths of our being which Simone Weil spoke of, revealed
that we might know the truth and be set free.

Péguy as poet did more than most men have ever presumed to
do in putting words into the mouth of God. As a teacher of
prayer he did more than most to make clear how and why it is
that silence alone can bear the full weight of what is attempted in
praying. He had dared to speak of God's need because he attached such meaning to freedom and love. 'Our consent is
necessary', wrote Simone Weil 'in order that He may perform
His own creation through us.' It was that creative thrust of the
Spirit that demanded silence for its true reception. To adapt St.
Paul's words, there are all kinds of silence and none of them is
without significance, but the silence that Péguy sought was that
which permitted the conjunction of the eternal and temporal to
be renewed. There was, if we may use W. H. Hudson's description of his experience in the great solitude of Patagonia, a silence
into which in rare conditions a human being might return, in
which the noisy engine of the mind was stilled, in which it seemed that the creation itself waited for the signal to go forward. It

was such a silence of expectation that Péguy knew.

'The faith and the love and the hope are all in the waiting.'

The importance of silence has been recognised by religious and mystics, by a spiritual élite, all down the ages. Péguy disliked élites and struggled throughout his life to speak and write for all sorts and conditions of men. His use of silence needs to be seen therefore in relation to the whole course of that common life. His aim was to move more deeply into it, not away from it. He sought therefore to make full use of the silence that causes the fanciful to wither away so that the authentic relationships might be freed from the spurious. Only in such a silence, not measured by time, could such a purgation be effected. There is a moment in the story of Mr Weston's *Good Wine* when a strange and un-looked for event suddenly happens; 'Time be stopped', exclaim-ed Mr. Bunce excitedly. 'And eternity have begun' said Mr. Grunter. It was not perhaps the most accurate way of describing it but it did make clear that at such a moment things might be seen in a different light. How different only those involved might know. Things suddenly uncovered might shock or ex-hilarate, appal or gladden, the eyes now opened at such a time. Seeming at least would be dissolved. Consider it for a moment as it occurs in Hamlet. The death of fathers is being talked of, the common event is agreed on. Then Gertrude makes the remark 'Why seems it so particular with thee?' and time stops. We need one moment of the eternal silence to hear and digest Hamlet's reply, 'Seems, Madam, nay, it is'.

Of the many kinds of silence what is it then that Péguy most deliberately points us to? The peremptory 'procure silence' of Kierkegaard's advice may easily lend itself to becoming no more than the voice of an usher in a Court of Law or the order of some official that we should lay our hand upon our mouth as a sign of respect for Majesty. The custom is old and common enough in human history to lend itself to the religious life and thereby help to make it all too often, in Buber's words 'an obstacle to the life lived in the spirit'. Majesty there is, majesty beyond telling that must rightly evoke awe and wonder, but not the majesty of emperors and kings whose magnificence like that of Solomon

commands gaping and breathless admiration. Majesty revealed in
the person of Jesus Christ points elsewhere, to a crown and a
throne and a state of another kind.

Buber has described the fundamental play of human life as the
two-fold action of setting at a distance and drawing into relation.
In that action silence has a considerable part to play. The
necessary conjunction of time and eternity fundamental to
Péguy's vision becomes in personal terms the relation of Thou
and I, pitching the tent of the Spirit in the space between man
and man, between Man and God. Silence is needed because 'only
silence before the Thou-silence of all tongues, silent patience in
the undivided word that precedes the formed and vocal response
– leaves the Thou free, and permits man to take his stand with it
in the reserve where the spirit is not manifest but is'. In that
silence not only is the bar between life and life removed but a
revelation is effected which is 'no thing among things, no event
among events' but a supra-personal act of recognition. Without
silence there can be no release from the gravitation of all things
to the condition of It. Communion itself is rendered impossible
and speech becomes no more than a filling up with words of
what threatens to become an intolerable gap. 'One formulates
these phrases,' said Johan, in Bergman's *Six Scenes in a Marriage*,
'to combat the void'. Decreation, a theme constantly in Péguy's
mind, thus enters the world between man and God. The drawing
into relation cannot take place for there is no silence to give
room to it.

'My soul is even as a weaned child.' In the Psalmist's words lies
yet another picture of the kind of silence we must seek. It carries
a strange message but is no stranger than the act of weaning.
Painters and poets down the ages have made the picture of the
child at the mother's breast one of the moving scenes of human
life. How deeply this contact of mother and child in the nur-
turing act affects the whole course of human life is something
that psychologists today in a great many ways acknowledge. No
less the act of weaning. Perhaps we have hardly begun to understand what things are consequential on that break. In the life to be
lived in the spirit it is we ourselves who must make it. The

process is something prolonged through life and something we only sustain by learning to be silent at deeper levels of being. For the nurturing of one person by another is not brought to an end in weaning but raised to a new level, to make way for an infinitely diverse set of relationships and to enable the richest growth to take place.

It is in the matter of speaking that this is put to the test. We grow up as children of our mother-tongue, learning to use it so easily and so carelessly that its soiled condition, its debasement by corrupt usage, escapes our knowledge and our ability to withstand it. The character of gossip to which we have referred has with the development of global mass-media so charged the atmosphere that it has been said with truth that 'we live in a wind-tunnel of gossip that reaches from theology and politics to an unprecedented noising of private concerns'. A lack of, even a deliberate assault upon reticence has become one of the marked features of our culture. 'Our dreams are marketed wholesale.' Words, the potential 'under-agents of the soul' are made the instruments of corruption and to dwell among people of unclean lips is, as the Hebrew prophets knew, to be exposed to a contamination that penetrates to the springs of human life. It is not with the grosser forms of such perverse use of language that we are solely concerned but with the most widespread reduction of words to an impersonal usage. 'After Auschwitz no poetry' for no words can sustain such defilement of human relations. Language becomes in its turn an exercise in despiritualisation of mankind. The steady devaluation of the word in the 20th century may well prove to be its most fundamental crisis. A new vision of Hell is conjured up in perceiving a state where no-one ceases to talk and no-one listens.

Péguy loved words as a craftsman, as teacher, as poet and as man of prayer. Much of his work was a battle on their behalf. He knew how words stood in relation to the spirit.

> The heart could never speak
> But that the Word was spoken.

His insistence upon beginning again as the heart of all spiritual life applied directly to the redemption of the word. To learn to be silent in the presence of words, to be courteous and chaste in relation to them, was a task which only silence could enable a man to undertake. It was the preliminary and the accompanying work of all prayer, a retracing of steps to the childhood of such speech, a constant purification of something committed to our charge. Words came so easily to men's lips and crowded so noisily into their consciousness that without making the effort to find silence there could be no relationships between them and God or between men themselves which was were not too heavy with reverberations to permit communication to take place. Silence was needed in which to renounce the too facile words that, like Legion, claimed to possess a man's soul.

3. Holy Ground

'Orléans qui êtes au pays de Loire.'
  Péguy, *Mystère de la Charité de Jeanne d'Arc.*
'He came to Nazareth where He had been brought up.'
                                                    The Gospel according to St. Luke.
'Earth is your talent. Use it.'
                                                    C. Day-Lewis, *New Year's Eve.*

Why does so much of our praying wither away? Why does this
secret ladder so often fade into unreality and vanish, giving us no
further help in spiritual life? One reason may be that our praying
too often and to too large an extent lacks earth to nourish it. Our
ladder lacks ground to stand upon. We are not unaware of the
fact that our lives in the modern Europeanised world have been
cut off from the natural earth to an extent unknown to earlier
generations but we have not always seen this as a spiritual
problem. Our prayer reflecting rather than challenging such a
condition has all too often begun and remained in a world of
abstractions. We have hardly dared turn in a different direction.

Much of our religious tradition has made things worse by putting the emphasis in our approach to God upon a renunciation of
concern for created things, upon a turning away from the world
that our senses make us aware of. It encouraged much self-decep-
tion. We affected concern but did not in truth really have it. Our
concern for the world was often too shallow to make it a matter
of spiritual choice at all. We proposed to abstain from what we
had never known. The result was clear. Our spirituality has been
to a disastrous extent precociously metaphysical. We have lacked
the sap of the earth to give life to our dealings with Heaven.

To have done so is to have squandered our resources and

50

neglected to use talents entrusted to us. As all prodigals must we
need to come to our senses again. As victims of pride we need to
be humbled by these so-called lowlier things.

> Pull down thy vanity, I say pull down.
> Learn of the green world what can be thy place
> In scaled invention or true artistry,
> Pull down thy vanity,
>   Paquin pull down.
> The green casque has outdone your elegance. [1]

All of us need to learn what it means to be of the earth earthy if
we are to grow up to our full stature as the children of God. We
cannot, except to our own undoing, ignore or bypass the earth
and the earth-bound ties which God has knit to Himself in love.
To treat His creation as if it were no more than a snare or an
irrelevance is from the outset to defame Him. We shall not learn
to know Him aright or to honour His name or to rejoice in His
splendour if we grow so dull as to fail to perceive how the
heavens declare His glory or grow deaf to the trees of the wood.
The salvation we look for is, in the terms of the Bible itself, inex-
tricably bound up with the fate and future of all the creation. A
resolute seeking for Him who made all things must compel us to
honour the things He has made. The gods of the pagans were not
dethroned to leave the earth bereft of glory, but that we with
new-opened eyes might more purely and more extensively
worship its Maker, releasing the currents of adoration from the
rockpools of pagan awareness that they might flow freely
towards the God of all Gods. With nature we share in the pangs
of both birth and death, in the quickening of growth and matur-
ing of fruit; with nature no less we look for redemption.

Yet we find ourselves greatly at odds with our world. This is
not the only sphere in which our frequent undoing springs from
a putting asunder of that which He has joined together, but it is a
grievous example of it. It is one that threatens to damage, con-

1. Ezra Pound, Cantos − Canto LXXXI.

ceivably to destroy us all, the more our urbanised life and 'our conquests of nature' define more straitly our sophisticated modes of living'. 'Never before,' wrote Herbert Read, 'in the history of the Western World has the divorce between man and nature, between man and his fellow-man, between the individual man and his selfhood been so complete'. Estrangement from ourselves must squander all our resources in internal warfare, estrangement from others rob us of our capacity to become persons at all, but that which divides us from nature must mean to an ever-increasing extent the loss of a power to respond, to delight in, to wonder. It must dry up the springs of worship.

Much folly has been indulged in since Rousseau and others invited mankind to attend to nature, and becoming self-conscious about it, made a cult of its more amenable aspects. The cult or cults remained on the fringe of the vast economic technological changes that produced a new world and equally on the fringe of religion. Industrial and commercial powers proceeded to ravage the earth as never before while religion clung to its traditional modes of expressing the relations of God and man. The questions that such changes in man's use of and relation to the earth should have been seen to raise were not set clearly before men's hearts and minds by Churches too frightened by the revolution and too ill-equipped by their past history to be greatly serviceable to God or man. It fell rather to men outside the established churches to raise their voices about the natural world and their voices were divided. It would be wrong to dismiss them as wholly ineffective. Their protests remained and in time were listened to. Their pleas for more 'natural' life gained respect. There would come a time when schoolchildren − a new feature in life − would be permitted not only to learn 3Rs but also to paint a flower, still later to handle clay! There would be some men who opened parks in the cities to give working-class people a glimpse of beauty, though 'not during the hour of Divine service'. In time the idea of a garden village would compete for attention in the building of cities and be acted on. Religion would be affected but change here would be very slow.

We must pause on this if we are to understand our own

spiritual poverty. A disastrous split in consciousness could not but
have deplorable results. The more fortunate few were free to
make use of access to nature. Like Wordsworth they might
cultivate enjoyment of experience of a largely unspoiled world,
like Thoreau they might turn their backs upon the cities and live
simple lives in the woods. Like Gilbert White and W.H. Hudson
they might learn to observe with passionate care the diversities of
natural beauty always within reach. But for the great masses of
people there was limited access to such things and little to open
their eyes by way of teaching about them. Men need to be taught
to see and their established guides were horribly blind. Men need
to be helped to develop and use their senses but their teachers
were all too often afraid of the senses themselves. So neither
mystical vision nor the free childlike delight in the sensuous
world were encouraged to grow in their lives. Generations of
maimed human beings resulted. The marvel is that the blind
guides were ever thrust aside and that some men and women at
least began to see with their eyes and hear with their ears what
the world of nature was like. When more affluent standards of
living came the deprived were more plainly lost. 'In the circumstances, it was not unusual for people to run outside and
jump into their cars. All of a Sunday they would visit, or be
visited, though sometimes they would cross one another,
midway, while remaining unaware of it. Then, on finding
nothing at the end, they would drive around, or around. They
would drive and look for something to look at'.

Neither the Wordsworthian nor the Thoreau-like cult of
nature is what we need. Great poet as he was, Wordsworth
nevertheless fell victim to limitations of a personal kind as
William Blake hinted. He stopped short at the sight of the
natural world and lost the still greater vision that that world
should have trained him to see. He had known and was able to
write of those moments when

> the visible scene
> Would enter unawares into his mind,
> With all its solemn imagery, its rocks,

Its woods, and that uncertain heaven, received
Into the bosom of the steady lake.

but he was not able to advance beyond them. He chose rather to
try to make a creed called 'natural piety' out of his vision, argu-
ing that the individual mind (and the progressive powers perhaps
no less of the whole species) were 'fitted' to the external world.
He meant by that that nature and the human spirit were in some
kind of harmony, and that his own experience of the 'sentiment
of Being spread o'er all that moves and all that seemeth still' was
sufficient evidence of this. It is noteworthy that Blake com-
mented, 'You shall not bring me down to believe such fitting and
fitted,' nor in the longer run did Wordsworth find it so. Natural
piety in the end would be, however respectably got up, no better
able to nourish the souls of men than the worship of Pan or
Astarte.

Yet it is with the earth of the countryside that we begin in learning to pray with Péguy. He lived as most of us do in cities and
he had no great desire to see the length and breadth of France or
the seas around it, much less of the world beyond. He would no
doubt have agreed with Thoreau that it was not worth while to
go round the world to count the cats in Zanzibar. But townsman
though he was, he did not lose sight of the fields and villages
from which his people came. Solidarity with that people was
always a commanding factor in his mind and he knew that it was
rooted in the soil. As he grew older and more mature as a poet he
gave more and more attention to it. But it was by no means
'natural piety' nor was it mystical vision of a Wordsworthian
kind that was shaped by that attention. It was not nature apart
from man as some of the nature enthusiasts were inclined to
revere, but a countryside worked by men's hands for some thir-
teen centuries and on which they had planted their villages and
homes. His mysteries beginning with that of Joan of Arc were
planted solidly in and among the meadows, wheatfields and
vineyards of Lorraine and the Île de France. It was as a homeland
that he thought of it, and Halévy comments 'the function of a
homeland is not to complete a man but to shape him for a higher

destiny'. The earth to Péguy is always a cradle, and as such respected and loved, but cradles are meant to be left behind. Nature-worshippers were moved to set up the cradle; Péguy knew better than that and insisted on planting a cross in the countryside as firmly as the peasants planted the seed. He took wayside crosses to symbolise most of what he loved in the earth itself.

But as always he was in no hurry to go beyond the carnal cradle. To many he was exasperatingly slow. But nothing better reveals the stuff of Péguy's spirituality than this laboured tenacious handling of the earth.

> Earth hard as justice, level as a table,
> Even as a cross-bar, as law equitable,
> Like a pond enclosed and yet open like a plinth.

and the equally harsh note of physical tiredness and hunger that accompanies it. This country 'flatter than the flattest table' seems to yield little at first sight to the eye in things that stir the heart, but Péguy was never a man to be greatly impressed by first sights. All his life was spent in going beyond them. As his poetry matured his attention moved nearer to the soil but was never halted there, and had his homeland been the Cévennes or the Auvergne rather than the flat Beauce he would not have been arrested by the mountains. The earth was shelter enough wherever it was rightly used.

The soil then was the starting place: soil of the garden planted by the Lord God in Eden and soil of the fields that men had wrested from the wild earth ever since – back-breaking sweat-soaked soil; soil of the earth trodden by Christ's feet and by all his saints and sinners; soil made the scene of His Passion and the covering of His burial, soil saturated with the tears and blood of His people down the years; soil the substance of man's body moulded to eat and drink and have children, and a marvellous subtle instrument compounded of clay to respond to the breath of God; soil of the fleshly house in which God's spirit was pleased to dwell, and soil to which the body would soon return.

We have added since Péguy's day a good deal to our knowledge of dust, as men's feet have stirred up the surface of the moon and their instruments have noted the clouds of interstellar dust, but always the thing that Péguy sought for remains to be seen. He was seeking a holiness in and through it. In the long poem *Eve,* he appears unwilling at times to turn away from or to cease trying to find words for this soil; 'this familiar earth', this primitive clay, this oozy slime, this soil of filth and dusty ore, this stuff of coal-seams and peat-beds, pastures and river banks. He would not leave it until he had used it to the fullest extent. There are many occasions when a very different poetic mind, that of Edwin Muir, strikes a similar note:

> Seek the beginnings, learn from whence you came,
> And know the various earths of which you are made.

It was utterly in keeping with Péguy's mind that he should carry that search for the beginnings right back to Eve herself, to Eve buried outside the primal garden, that he should listen to Jesus speaking:

> O mère ensevelie hors du premier jardin. [1]

and from that beginning see God Himself watching the unfolding of man's long journey:

> Et Dieu lui-même jeune ensemble qu'éternel
> Regardait ce que c'est que les pleurs du jeune âge.
> Integre il regardait d'un regard paternel
> Le monde commencer son long pèlerinage. [2]

The soil then bore the imprint of men's feet. It had a history

---

1. 'O mother entombed outside the primal garden.'
2. 'And God Himself, both young and eternal
   Notes that which is the tearfulness of youth.
   Looks justly and with father's care
   Upon a world, beginning its long pilgrimage.'

and for Péguy that was the dimension of active grace, the dimension of what he called God's eternal leap into the world, a frontal entry into the temporal. The soil had this ineffaceable character stamped upon it by the already long history of man's labouring on it:

> An endless reservoir for ages yet to come
> Two thousand years of work have conjured from this
>   soil;
> A thousand years of grace have conjured from this toil
> For solitary hearts an everlasting home.

So there was here something richer in content than natural piety and something more fitted to be what Péguy instinctively looked for, a *panem quotidianum,* a daily bread, formed from the commonplace things of man's working life and transformed by grace to be food for eternal life. One may not doubt the worth of flashes of mystical vision which have been to many a source of joy and wonder, moments of transfiguration, moments when barriers have dissolved and unions been effected, when the course of lives has been changed. Yet a need remains, as Robert Bridges put it:

> this glimpse or touch of immanence
> being a superlative brief moment of glory,
> is too little to leaven the inveterate lump of life.

and provision for that need was no less clear to Péguy. He grasped the soil because he believed that the leaven of grace was working in it and he prayed for mankind rooted in the soil as the heirs through Christ of eternal life

> Forgive them, O Lord,
> For loving so dearly their corruptible land.
> From it they were fashioned. Of this mud and this sand
> Was their primitive substance and scanty reward.

But Péguy went further than this because he was always 'making as if he would have gone further'. What came to him charged with such beauty must, he believed, be infinitely more prized by God. If men so loved their corruptible land, how much more must God love it also? So when he spoke of 'a kind of flavour of man, a kind of flavour of earth' that the Son brought back to Heaven, he not only echoed the cry of delight that old Isaac gave as the smell of the fields came to him from the supplanter who knelt before Him, but furnished an occasion for joy in the heart of God in tasting the flavour of the earth he had made and the earth His Son had redeemed, supplanting the old Supplanter. It was the kind of down-to-earth version of Browning's line, 'the gain of the earth must be Heaven's gain too' that Péguy was prepared to furnish. He knew a good deal about detachment and renunciation. They played a great part in the manner of life he chose to follow. He also knew that detachment might mean very little unless man had learned first to be attached with the cords of authentic love, that renunciation must have more than superficialities to renounce.

In a sermon entitled 'Nature, also, Mourns for a Lost Good', Tillich asked the question, 'Are we still able to understand what a sacrament means?' He asked it as part of a more general questioning of what nature now means to us, in itself and within the drama of man's salvation. He went on to say that the more estranged men grew from the natural world the less able they were to find meaning in sacraments at all. No remedy lay in efforts to heighten the consciousness of one or two such sacraments set apart. Men stood to lose what the sacramental understanding of life afforded if sacraments got detached from the common earth, if that most earth-bound gift of Himself by Christ was severed from field and vineyard, from the labours of men in the work of the world. We face such a question that touches the way we pray very deeply at a time when the fellowship aspect of the Holy Communion has probably gained greater weight of appeal than others, when to some christians it seems that the social concern has obscured a relation to God, when the emphasis placed upon it may reflect more misgivings about society than a hopeful and brave participation in it.

The question forces us back to the estrangements we have already mentioned and to a recognition of their indivisibility. What Tillich calls an understanding of a sacrament must mean not something complete but something itself being changed, being deepened, being carried further by those who are taking it into their lives. To 'use' a sacrament is to expose ourselves to the winds of change, to evince a willingness to be disturbed within and without ourselves by pressures we may not like. In a world where the pressures of nature have been so handled to conform to our business needs it may well be that we understand sacraments less and less.

In Péguy's work the sacramental sense is all-embracing. The countryside is a *milieu divin* not in any easy sense but as if charged with the redemptive activity of God. He was not writing poetry of the topographical kind that in english anthologies once made Adlestrop and Grantchester pleasant places, nor was he lingering over natural beauties to offset the smoke of cities. It was the immensely complicated structure of human enterprise, mines and forests, workshops and markets in and through which the world's economy and man's redemption were carried out and the two were not to be forced apart. Péguy held towns and countryside together. Paris he hailed as a great vessel moored beneath Notre Dame, a warship, a freighter, a galley, laden with all that men's skill through the years had produced. But who else would have sung with like fervour the sprawling *banlieue*? Kipling had chanted the romance of steam and Chesterton had dressed up Notting Hill to give reins to fancy, but Péguy was not trying to be romantic about either past or present conditions of the city. Geneviève in Paris like Joan in Domrémy stands not on romantic but on holy ground:

> et l'arbre de la grace est raciné profond
> et plonge dans le sol et cherche jusqu'au fond
> et l'arbre de la race est lui-même éternel. [1]

1. 'And the tree of grace has deep-thrusting roots,
    And drives through the soil and searches the depths,
    And the tree of the race is itself eternal.'

There was no doubt in Peguy's mind where that tree was rooted and he could be very explicit about it. In Walt Whitmanlike fashion he listed the things that he believed the Eternal Father loved, not only the souls of men but men at work in the fields and forests and women who washed and baked and dusted, lit the lamps on the kitchen tables and set out the meal, who arranged the flowers and tidied things up, and would do the same for God did He choose to call at the door.

Simplicity? Péguy saw it all with such eyes. He had as much anguished sense of God's hiddenness as Pascal himself, but he also had because he prayed much, and it was without doubt the greatest of all his gifts, a joyous awareness of God's delight in the world He had made. Blake only among the poets of Britain knew so completely that 'everything that lives is holy', and not even Blake could picture with such native-born delight when the days of Innocence were past, the home-coming of earth's children in the final dawn, treading their way through the thyme and lavender, the fumitory and the cornflowers, past the bakery and the village windmill, the orchards and the forge, presenting them all as holy to the Lord.

Such a vision was not the town-dweller's dream of a landscape to take refuge in nor was it a pagan pleasure that ignored the throes of the conflicts to be faced. Péguy looked at the soil of France with the eyes of both soldier and peasant. He was very conscious of the battlefields of the past, of the countryside he knew as breakwaters which had once withstood the tides of heathen invasion, and of the imminence of invasion yet again. For some fifteen centuries that part of France had known both the terrors of destruction and the exuberance of creative effort. Men and women had bent their backs to subdue the soil, taking droughts and disease as part of the cost, seen their work plundered and ruined by war, and set about doing it over again.

Péguy's poetry of that countryside invites comparison with that of Hardy and the peculiar nature of the frenchman's work is clear enough. He pays no attention to the ironies of circumstance, the reflections of women and men about each other, the personal faults or traits of character. It is not that he is less humanly concerned, less conscious of pain and love, but that his vision has more in keeping with the perspective of the *Dynasts* than with the poetry of the Wessex villages. But then the contrast sharpens for it is no President of the Immortals nor shadowy Spirits of Pity and the Years that survey the human scene but the God and Father of Jesus Christ and the company of Saints. They are involved in all that happens. Hardy could write of an earth long -since forgotten by its Maker; Péguy would always reply that it was not written that God would abandon His people. He watched and waited and helped where He could like a human father, careful to cherish freedom, concerned above all with true growth.

Such vision did not exclude appreciation of the old pagan world nor lessen his admiration of a poet like Victor Hugo as of one who had 'the gift of seeing the creation as if it came that morning out of the Creator's hands'. But he himself stood, like Edwin Muir, 'one foot in Eden' and looked at the other land, conscious that that bright beauty of the primal world lacked something which the most woe-begone christian might perceive when with the eyes of faith he saw at some time in his life the great ladder set up on the earth and God's dealings with men made plain. Péguy's sacramentalism flowed from an unassailable conviction of the Incarnation as 'the still centre of the turning world', and from a here and now understanding of it. 'God Himself culminates in the present moment, and will never be more divine in the lapse of all the ages.' In that nutshell kingdom that lay between Paris, Orléans and Chartres he could count himself more than a king of infinite space, a frenchman and a child of God.

He needed no more. Péguy's delight in the Creation is inseparable from his pride in being a Frenchman. God speaks . . .

> Et je reconnais ici la résonnance et le rang du Français
> Et je salue
> leur ordre propre.
> Peuple à qui les plus grandes grandeurs
> Sont ordinaires.

Je salue ici ta liberté, ta grâce,
Ta courtoisie. [1]

We should do Péguy wrong and miss the real point of his work
if we read what he said about Frenchmen in terms of a stupid
nationalistic pride. Few men have spent more of their energy in
attacking things done and said by their countrymen in their
country's name than Péguy. His love for France was of that
quality that detected and resented the least stain upon the honour
of the nation. There were times when like the Psalmist again he
groaned aloud that 'they are altogether gone out of the way'.
The Third Republic was no lovely sight in the eyes of one who
cared so deeply for the purity of a nation's life. He would have it
above suspicion, so he fought all his life on its behalf. He knew
that its faults were not redeemed by insolence however pious or
by thoughtless repetition of patriotic hymns. Above all he insisted that France must be synonymous with freedom.
Frenchmen, says God, know what freedom means.

It is of course but a hairsbreadth from arrogance and sin lies at
the door, but we must read it as Péguy's prayer, as the never-
to-be quenched thirst for the salvation of a people.

> O people inventors of the Cathedral, I have in nowise found
> you light in faith.
> O people inventors of the Crusade, I have in nowise found
> you light in charity.

> As for hope, we had better not talk of it, there is no-one
> like them for that.

When he names their virtues he does so not because he is satisfied that they possess them by right but because he must summon

1. 'And I acknowledge the impact and the place of Frenchmen,
   And I salute
   Their fitting warranty.
   People to whom the highest heights
   Are common.
   I salute your freedom, your grace,
   Your courtesy.'

them to fight for them. Much of his comment was a tireless searching out of the things that mattered to mankind which had been fought for on the soil of France. He thought of this people's tireless pursuit of freedom, 'not an intellectual, conceptual, bookish liberty, a ready-made liberty, a codified liberty, but a primitive organic, living liberty'. It is not difficult to choke with objections to Péguy's historical judgments, to recall the Wars of Religion, the royal absolutism, the aristocratic tyranny, the oppression and near-starvation of workers in town and countryside.

But Péguy did not forget or ignore such things. He called them quite plainly sins. He approached the social conditions of every régime with a person in mind, a person he knew, the father of children, himself. It was these 'most engaged' men of the world these most exposed to the storms, that he made his standard of judgment. 'What do wars and revolutions, civil and foreign wars, the future of society, the fall of a people, mean to others? They risk nothing but their heads . . . but he, the father of the family, is not only engaged in the present, and in the past, in memory and history, but assailed by scruples, stung by remorse in advance at the thought of the city of tomorrow, of the dissolution and decadence and the failure of a people to whom he is committing his children in a few years time'. It was because Péguy engaged himself and his family in that way for the sake of the people of France and the world that he can teach us much about prayer.

On that soil of France he did the unfashionable but quite characteristic thing of making a pilgrimage to Chartres. Some of his most moving poetry commemorates that journey. He presented the Beauce to Our Lady of Chartres. It was hers already by age-long right but Péguy meant the acknowledgment to confirm her title as a gesture of gratitude and of hope. 'The earth is the Lord's' – the truth could never be named too often, but that special bit belonged to the Queen and that too needed to be said again. A pilgrimage gets to the holy place at last but what gives it its part in prayer is the slamming down of one's feet to complete the journey praying the while for all its features. A child of that countryside he trod out the kilometres that brought him at length to the sight of that spire — *le plus beau fleuron dedans votre couronne* — with the joyfulness of a lover, the delight of an artist, the ecstasy of one who worships. The groundwork of his prayer was the rippling ocean of wheat, the bright gold of broom, the dignity of poplars, the gaiety of apple-orchards, the arabesque of the sandy Loire. There is a story told of him that as a child he refused to run out and join a crowd in the street who were watching a calf 'because he had to finish his map of France'. In truth, he could never finish that map, not even the narrowed-down bit he trod out because it was inexhaustibly rich.

He would come at last to Chartres. 'Like all great churches that are not mere storehouses of theology, Chartres expressed, beside whatever else it meant, an emotion, the deepest man ever felt, — the struggle of his own littleness to grasp the infinite'. So Henry Adams wrote, and perhaps no writer of english has said better what Chartres is and means to men, confessing that all human work ends there, so that in times to come men will no doubt do it differently but not better, will speak as clearly in their different tongues, but not say more than this.

> This is the stone without a stain, or fault
> Never was a prayer that carried greater weight,
> And never was an argument that went more straight,
> And never taller line soared to a boundless vault.

As Martin Johnson wrote of the sculpture of Chartres there is in the whole work the record of a gigantic act of imaginative faith 'from which much might be derived for the mid-twentieth century'. He went on to say: 'The figures themselves confront us, and will continue to confront our descendents with the question: "Can you endure the terror we have known and attain the Vision Splendid which only our strength of mind can give?' Péguy understood that the cathedrals of the Ile de France expressed that intuitive grasp or insight in which, if for a brief moment only in man's long journey through the night, it might be said in truth that God and man had seen through the same eye.

He came to Chartres from that other Notre Dame whose glory

he celebrated in other poems. He carried with him the thought of
Beauvais, Cambrai, Amiens, Rheims and saw them all in the imagery of an ear of corn resistant to scorching and frost alike, lifted
up by the hands of men who had 'learned to know their way and
what it is to choose', the blossoming of the dust itself before the
feet of her who so perfectly knew the needs of men. Between
Notre Dame de Paris and Notre Dame de Chartres Péguy drew a
base line from which to survey all human life, measuring it with
his feet as carefully as the Christ had done in His going up and
down to the Holy City. The base line of all true vision must be
the earth so painstakingly measured out, its intersection with the
Eternal never out of mind, its accumulation of joy and sorrow
always in sight. It was the base court of the Holy City and needed to be known as such. Only so would the soil of the earth be
rightly used. There is, in Shakespeare's Richard II, a crucial moment when the king puts off his majesty and state to come down
to the base court. The King of Kings Himself had so descended,
and our ladder of prayer to have any base at all must be located
there, on the ground He has consecrated to Himself for ever.

> God bless the ground. I shall walk softly there,
> And learn by going where I have to go.

Praying is concerned with getting things right in the scale of
what truly matters to mankind. Day after day it must endeavour
to redraw the picture, correcting the distortions, perceiving new
immensities, making sharper and clearer what is becoming
obscured. What Péguy had to teach about prayer sprang from
what must be called the faithful freedom of his eyes. He kept it
by keeping the holy ground in view. He went on looking at the
soil of France and a good deal of his writing about it resembles
nothing so much as rubbing his eyes to look at it again. He felt
free to do so because that soil spelled out to him a message of
human freedom. He looked at the Church and the World less
hampered by those forms which in art and politics, religion and
work provide for men the conventions of seeing than most of his
contemporaries. He walked by faith which meant being ready to
do without the rules of pre-conceived design and his freedom

shocked many who adhered and required adherence to them. 'The liberty of the creature is the most beautiful reflection,' he wrote, 'of the Liberty of the Creator'. He went on to ask what use or value could be attached to the beatitude of slaves. It was no rhetorical question but the mainspring of his life, the conviction which made him challenge whatever threatened to curtail human freedom. His Joan, his de Joinville, his St. Louis and all his soldier saints were loved because they were in his estimation free. Where he differed from many another christian was made clear in a comment of Julian Green's describing one such 'as a truly christian soul in catholic armour, an armour that hampers his movements'. The faith by which Péguy lived had no better illustration than David's stripping off Saul's armour before going out to meet Goliath.

Sacramental vision is not instant photography of the world in which we live. It is something learned by the patient education of our sensibility to the engagement of God with the world. 'It has called for nothing less than the whole earth to produce man,' wrote Teilhard de Chardin, 'and the real man is the man who gathers, or will gather, within himself, the consciousness of the whole human stratum ... By means of all created things, without exception, the divine assails us, penetrates us, moulds us. We imagined it as distant and inaccessible, whereas we live steeped in it'. It was a part of Péguy's task to recover men to such an awareness of that encompassing presence of God. He was well aware that such contemplation was not all that was demanded of the christian but he believed that without such a sense of the holiness of the earth he stood upon he would lose even the will to respond to God. 'Why stay we on the earth unless to grow?' Is the dying of the light so trivial a matter that we need not notice it? Is the dawn so commonplace that we can do no more than yawn upon it?

> How annoying, God says; When there are no more Frenchmen,
> There are things which I do, nobody will any longer understand.

4. 'Mes Vieilles Paroisses Francaises'

'A Christianity which has given up the mediation of work and the world as a constituent core of faith and can only reintroduce it later at a secondary, derivative level, can only falsify both the gospel and man's most authentic experience.'

José. M. Bonino, *Revolutionary Theology comes of Age.*

'O people that I have loved, shall we not answer together?'

Padraic Pearse, *The Fool.*

Do you pray the parish? The question may strike you as odd, meaningless, and in the light of what is to be said later, perversely posed. But it has to be asked and taken as a supremely important question with which all our reflections upon the life of the christian Church in the world, including its survival, and upon prayer itself, are deeply concerned. It has to do with that gigantic revolution which in the last two hundred years has completely changed the conditions of human life throughout the world and is doing so now at an ever-increasing rate. It is the change manifest in the scientific and technological revolutions, in the growing urbanisation of mankind, in the rise of Socialism and of movements to achieve colonial emancipation, in the overthrow of old Empires and the rise, to power of new ones in the form of multi-national companies, and the bearing of all these things upon the ancient small communities of the Christian Church called parishes.

Such a question does not commonly appear in books on prayer, and until quite recently had made little impact upon theology. Ten years after Vatican II it is no longer possible to ignore such questions or to dismiss the Theology of Liberation as a

67

wild aberration, but neither is it clear that the Churches have so shaken themselves free from fear and from a reluctance to change their attitudes towards the world that they are able to address themselves hopefully to a radical reshaping of their structures, thinking, policies and modes of life. That they are disturbed is obvious enough, but what matters most, and what concerns us here, is the extent to which a sorrowing after a godly sort and an expectation of divine guidance has entered into and changed our ways of praying with particular reference to the parish itself. Missions and ministries of an extra-parochial nature have gained considerable support, but while some changes have been made and even enforced by financial considerations upon the structure of the parochial ministry it can hardly be said that the whole nature of the problem presented by the present state of the parishes has been recognised and taken to heart.

Set the question with which we began along with others like 'praying the Mass', or 'praying your theology' or 'praying your life' and ask it again. We may have replied already that we pray for our friends and neighbours, for the local community in which we live, for the Church and the nation to which we belong, for the world itself with its many problems, and that in all this we pray thankfully for the help and support they give us as well for the various needs of those who are sick, estranged, hurt, burdened and in misery. All this requires much effort.

But our question implies something more. It is concerned with the way in which we ourselves are related to each other as Christians and as human beings, with the way in which we are all enmeshed in a social life which shapes to a large extent how we live and think and regard each other. It is the world of our assumptions, the world which makes us speak with a certain tone of voice to some and not to others, the world which we take for granted in our scale of values. Our question requires us to examine this world in the most searching fashion. There is a disagreeable phrase in the Psalms about people 'enclosed in their own fat' and whose mouths as a consequence speak 'proud things'. We recall how plainly Jesus Christ described the inability of some men who made long prayers to see the kind of assumptions from within which they prayed and the outcome of this in their praying. We are required to scrutinise and ask questions about this world as deliberately, for example, as some aids to praying direct our attention to the ways in which we dispose our bodies and breathing when we endeavour to pray. What are the marks of this society in which we live? How far is it unified or divided, and upon what basis? In what ways is it oppressive to some, indulgent to others, and why? Who are its deprived and needy, and why are they so?

At this point the parish is the focus of such questioning, that is to say, the immediate nexus of relationships from which we start. 'Human beings', wrote Maurice Nédoncelle in his book *The Nature and Use of Prayer*, 'cannot, while they live, be rid of life. They cannot so spiritualise their relationship that it becomes immaterial, an exchange between two centres of disembodied freedom'. We can go further and say that we cannot so spiritualise our relation with God that it takes no account of our bodies and His. He is and remains a Hidden God but 'that which we have seen and heard, that which we have handled' is the bond between us. He has taken our flesh, taken our manhood into Godhead, so that no aspect of this material world and of its unfolding history can be unimportant to Him. 'Eternity is in love with the productions of time.'

That love is of such a character that all that men can hope to do in their response is through the channels of adoration to reflect upon it and reflect its nature in their own lives. No aspect of it can be unimportant to them. They are set free from the limitations of both a godless and demon infested world that they may honour and use freely those things which have been made the channels of His grace and the flesh of His Body. Sensible supports are the springboard to enable the man who prays to go further, to penetrate more deeply into the things of God. They are the ladder entrusted to our use. They are set down because our very limitations require it in the immediate circumstances of our lives in society, and we must needs ask ourselves to what extent our praying gladly embraces this fact or endeavours to step outside this involvement, seeking to exclude it as a turbulent distracting thing which for our own peace of mind we would willingly put by. Or do we see it, albeit with pain and travail of soul, as stuff in which something called the common life in the Body of Christ is being formed, in which that Body is present to be honoured or rejected, loved or hated, now in this time of our mortal life?

Charles Dickens began his literary career with the sentence – 'How much is conveyed in those two short words – The Parish'. Boz went on to describe the conditions of poverty and squalor, of ill-usage and cruelty, that were associated with it. In the social history of yesterday's England the parish meant for great numbers of men and women the Poor Law and the beadle. It meant also something which caused a clerical novelist like Francis Paget to exclaim, 'Turn where you will, there stands at a distance of two or three miles from each other a church. Think what that implies. The Priest! The man of education! One household at least in every parish which shall be setting a good example and shedding a humanising influence around.' It was an idealised picture no doubt but it pointed to what Coleridge called 'this unobtrusive continuous agency – that to every parish throughout the kingdom there is transplanted a germ of civilisation; that in the remotest villages there is a nucleus round which the capabilities of the place may crystallise and brighten'. It represented in however a shrunken form what Christendom had meant to Europe, a rootedness in the soil of the christian gospel, a gathering into one conspectus of life all aspects of human experience in each place.

That it has all but died is clear enough today. In towns and cities and much of the countryside, the parish today is almost a meaningless term. Parochial is a pejorative word, expressive of self-centred, unimaginative, mean and narrowed vision. What remains of it in ecclesiastical forms works badly, hampering and discouraging both laity and clergy who hope for something better. It is clear that for far too long the Church and Churches, have acquiesced in structures which failed lamentably to promote either effective teaching or pastoral care. They simply did not reach the great masses of people in ways that impinged deeply upon their lives. Other agencies, to use Coleridge's word, have pushed the parish out of the picture and while we may well believe that none of them do what the parish once did, they function with greater impact upon men's minds and bodies. The field may be ill-nourishing to personal life but they hold it. The churches meanwhile have been forced to concern themselves with devotional services and a good deal of effort to find money to keep them going.

Do we gain very much then in trying to speak of the parish as one step in our ladder of prayer? Must we try to set about re-creating parishes of a newer sort that may bring the christian gospel into a more effective touch with the lives of people dispersed in the world today? Such questioning is inescapable. It has been pointed out already that such questions as 'What sort of society are we looking for?' and 'What kind of people are needed for the creation of this society?' do pose for christians at least the question 'What kind of church is needed to provide spiritual leadership in tomorrow's world?'. That in its turn brings us to the more fundamental matter of our praying, to the way in which we regard this relationship with others as setting the agenda for prayer itself. 'We need one another to be ourselves.' John MacMurray devoted a lifetime's work to trying to help men see that the fundamental fact of personal existence is our complete dependence upon others, the basic fact of our human condition. How much or how little of this has gone into praying the state of the parish may well record.

To turn to Péguy at this point, bearing in mind how carefully he chose words, is to be confronted with a startling comment. 'The chief thing that needs re-making,' he said, 'the most important of all, is the parish'. Halévy described that remark as 'pure Péguy', and went on to say, 'True peasant that he was, his concern was with those things that stood four-square on solid earth: the family, the workshop, the parish'. Today we can hardly help hearing the questionable overtones of Vichy in such words, but that apart, do they tell us what Péguy was really concerned with? Was it only the peasant in him that marked out the supreme importance of the parish, or was it Péguy saturated with both classical and christian culture, Péguy the revolutionary fighter, Péguy the wrestler with Christ, Péguy whose praying meant nothing so much as digging deeper the channels of Grace that they might run like rivers in spate through a thirsty land? Was it the man to whom communion spelled out the Gospel itself, to whom the embodiment of love meant living experience of community, to whom the 'carnal cradle' of Christ was the bedrock of devotion? As was to be expected he put the answer into the mouth of God:

> 'Et moi qu'est-ce que je serais sans mes vieilles paroisses françaises.
> Qu'est-ce que je deviendrais. C'est là que mon nom monte énternellement.'[1]

What would I do without my old French parishes?

It was no easily asked rhetorical question for Péguy was well aware that for a very long time God had had to do without them and that as far as the great towns and industrialised districts were concerned these 'old French parishes' as he conceived them had never existed. The name only remained, the substance was missing. 'Everything' he had said, 'depends upon embodiment, upon incarnation,' and he had looked to see the Church in the parish as the body of people in whom the Creative Word was taking flesh with infinite pain and humiliation yet with joy and hope. Et homo factus est. With that he began and endeavoured to stay. He had no illusions about men's sins in these parishes of old France but he believed that they were all carried and dealt with because the Christianisation was at work. The continuity of that embodiment of the Word though it might be at times abysmally slow and hard to perceive had nevertheless been assured.

Now it was all in jeopardy. A new world had come into being, shaping the lives of men in ways quite unforeseen and unprepared for, devouring their strength, assaulting their manhood,

1. 'And I myself, what should I be without my ancient french parishes? What would become of me? For there my name is raised eternally.'

and committing them to struggles of which the traditional Church knew nothing. Its influence was such that no part of the world, even to the most remote rural village, would be un-affected by it. In the face of this monde moderne the Church had continued to act as if it alone possessed the keys. It compromised with the rulers of this new world and turned a blind eye to the problems it dared not face. It trained its clergy upon traditional lines and sent them into this world quite unfitted to understand its problems. Inevitably such men had access to less and less significant areas of contemporary life.

As the tensions of this economic-political-social scene grew more profound the irrelevance of a clergy who at best endeavoured to ignore them became increasingly clear. The struggle of working-class people, by no means wholly political, but geared to a division of mankind between 'them' and 'us', pushed such clergy aside. In France it issued in bitter struggles between clerical and anti-clerical factions. In England where it took less spectacular forms it was closely recorded in the novel. What the rejection of the clergy was like is nowhere better described than in D. H. Lawrence's story *Daughters of the Vicar*. 'They were not very well received by the new, raw, disaffected population of colliers. Being accustomed to farm labourers, Mr. Lindley had considered himself as belonging to the upper or ordering classes. He found, however, that the collier population refused to accept this arrangement. They had no use for him in their lives, and they told him so callously'. Even where the social distinction was less marked, clerical training geared to a world that had vanished diverted attention from the aspirations and anxieties of a population compelled to be militant and suspicious. All too often the priests did not begin to see that the serious worker demanded something much more relevant to his situation than the theology to which they themselves were accustomed. They were quite unable to translate what they possessed into a language 'understanded of the people'. In the necessary ver-nacular of conflict they were dumb.

Péguy anticipated much that was to be said by outstanding priests like the Abbés Godin and Daniel and by Cardinal Suhard in the conflicts that raged round the Worker-Priests of the following years. In the prose writing now known as *Clio I*, found among Péguy's unpublished papers, he accused the clerks of having allowed themselves to become the agents of a process of de-christianisation, the outcome of which was to be seen in the emergence of a people 'profoundly, intimately, interiorly unchristian, de-christianised in heart and soul and marrow'. He spoke of this clerkly treason in terms of the loss of the parishes. 'The curés, my friend, have lost the people who had received the eternal promise.' He called it a disaster, this actual modern de-christianisation; 'the fact that such vast sections of humanity should never have been reached; that the invasion should never have begun; that there should have been so many blank patches in the parts attained and occupied'. With all the bitterness of Ezekiel he rounded upon the clerks. 'They abolish the mystery of creation itself. They remove creation, incarnation, redemption, merit, salvation and the value of salvation, judgement and much besides, and of course, above all, grace.'

Always, Péguy turned the matter into a question of prayer. In this case it was a prayer for the whole nation threatened with spiritual death, with the decay and loss of what had been its source of spiritual life. He refused to admit that the lostness was irrevocable, but its continuance, like the presence of the english soldiery in France at the time of Joan of Arc, was an open sore, a source of physical and spiritual anguish. He put into Joan's lament over the ravished state of Christendom the pain which he himself felt for the condition of the France he knew. There are moments in the poem *Eve* when he seems to choke over the wantonness of the betrayal, over the mood of *ennui* that has enveloped this once christian land; *notre morne ennui, notre énorme ennui, notre prude ennui* [1] . . . till the adjectives of disgust are exhausted. As we read it now we are bound to ask how far our prayer starts from this sense of pain, from this sense of lostness as a people.

---

1. 'our dejected weariness, our overwhelming boredom, our prudish vacuity.'

The battles between anti-clericals and clericals in the Third
Republic at the close of the 19th century and the beginning of the
20th, are so far from anything familiar to english minds that we
need to look closely at Péguy's position. He took no sides in the
conventional sense. With friends both atheist and catholic he
waged war upon catholics and atheists alike, tearing off the labels
that men took to themselves or fastened on others, laying bare the
real points at issue which the contestants so often concealed. He
loathed the readiness of both sides to resort simply to a struggle
for power. He struck with equal warmth at 'lay-curés who deny
the eternal aspect of the temporal' and at 'ecclesiastical curés who
deny the temporal in the eternal'. He reserved for the
ecclesiastical curés the special charge of failing to make known,
of even abolishing the mystery of creation. He saw them as men
who in their hearts despised the created order: 'the idea at the
back of their heads, is that the good God created the whole of his
creation, in which we are creatures, not only badly . . . but
pointlessly, emptily, which makes no sense at all'.

The christian operation he insisted, was turned towards the
world, a movement in and through the world to nourish it, to
renew it over and over again. God Himself moved into and
engaged Himself with that world, that His purpose might be
fulfilled. And this the clerks refused to see − 'it is not the laity
who withered and dried up' − setting their faces and minds
against the world they were charged to pray for. 'And then,' he
wrote bitterly, 'they give advice to the fathers of families, to the
men who bear the burden of life in the world, they walk with
horrifying brutality in the gardens of grace, you would think
they were enlisted to do nothing else. Elephant's feet in the gardens of the Lord'.

What then does the parish mean as we try to follow out the
line of Péguy's thought? Clearly it was no revival of the long-
vanished parish of Joan's Domrémy. To be rooted in the actual
world, the urbanised world of the day, it had to take note of and
respect the conditions of life, of the working life, of the men and
women concerned. It had to discover how the personal essence of
the lives of these people could best be aided and nourished in the

conditions in which they were found. Anything like an attempt to impose a parochial structure, new or old, was out of the question. Péguy had no blue-prints for the parish he prayed for. What mattered most was the measure of hunger and hope that a man or woman brought in praying towards the conception of the parish yet to be founded. Where most people either acquiesced in the state of affairs they saw or walked out and paid no further attention to it, Péguy did neither. He went on searching in prayer for the true lineaments of the parish-to-be. It is this which now must be seen as bearing upon the question with which this chapter began. To pray the parish as Péguy prayed it was a well-nigh intolerable burden, a going down the ladder into depths that brought pain and anguish throughout. 'By the waters of Babylon we sat down and wept.' It means nothing less than an unallayed thirst and hunger for that which we hope for, a rejection of false measures, a sifting and probing and waiting for what is valid, a silence that waits to hear, an active not passive attention.

The parish means a body of people drawn and held together in a spirit that prompts the members to care for, respect and love each other. It is the embodiment in any place of the I-in-You, You-in-Me relationship which Christ prayed for. Larger than the family which has its own special intimacies and responsibilities, the parish so conceived has the job of nurturing all its members that they may, in New Testament terms, grow up to their full stature in Christ. Something begun in the life of the family is to be carried into the next necessary stage of personal development. Small enough to permit a true understanding to grow up between its members such a body must extend their lives by confronting them with diversities of character and achievement, encouraging each person to be himself, relating each to a common life that is enriched by that which each supplies and yet is more than the sum of their gifts.

Such a body would ever be seeking to do two kinds of work; the one within itself in relating its members ever more genuinely to each other in love, the other in shaping a common attitude towards the life of the world in which it is set. Learning to speak the truth together in love, its members would form a community not withdrawn from but actively engaged with the world, and experiencing in an ever-deepening fashion a communion of transcendent character. It would see itself as the Church of Christ yet be ready to greet and work with others, sharing as far as it could the resources which it possessed. It would at all times be seeking with expectant hope to be able to experience more of the common life in the Body of Christ. Its prayer would be the quite natural breathing of the body thus engaged.

To describe it in this way should make clear that it lies within the reach of men and women willing to seek it, and that it does involve a radical change in the ways in which Churches now perform their functions: within reach because we can start at once, a radical change because it could forego the endless raising of money and the provision of devotional services which now occupies the greater part of the time and energy of Church-members acting together. It is radical in Péguy's sense, in the Old Testament sense of 'To your tents, O Israel', in the New Testament sense of taking seriously the health of the life of the Body.

Scattered among the people in our fragmented churches today there are those who hunger for something other than that they see, who are in pain because the church they belong to seems hopelessly stuck fast in a way of life that by no stretch of im- agination can be described in terms of leaven or salt or light, who realise daily that the words which are used to speak of the Church are far from being embodied in it. They know that the fellowship talked of does not take hold in a workmanlike way of the intricate fabric of human affairs nor confront the world in any decisive fashion. They are conscious that this church has real- ly no mind informed by the lively questioning of the experience of its members, no active will to address itself to unfamiliar problems. Somewhere beyond the boundaries of this local church the matters affecting all human life are being considered, pronouncements and reports are being made and commended to the churches, but these are not geared to receive them, not at- tuned to the job of making them the substance of their prayer and thought. The nervous system of this body transmits such messages feebly, maintains but clumsy continuity of attention, falls back upon pious responses and gets preoccupied with its own survival. Such people are conscious, as Péguy was, that the parish has been put into reverse.

Let us suppose then that such people get together, whether clergy or laity or both, for no other purpose than to try to find out what being a parish in process of renewal could mean at this present time, opening their hearts and minds to each other, making the communication between themselves and God of one piece throughout, facing the world in the most sensitive and fearless way and stringently examining their own conduct in it. In prayer both silent and voiced they are committed to expectation of rebirth. Let them decide to make this coming together and what it entails the priority of their conscious service of God. To use such words at all must make them at least uneasy and in that uneasiness they must learn to live. Péguy spoke often of it as invincible anxiety; while Abraham Heschel called it a sense of requiredness, in the language of the Bible: what is required of me? Let them hear in a personal fashion those Biblical words 'Come and I will send thee'. Or others of St Augustine: 'You are the Body of Christ, that is to say, in you and through you the method and work of the Incarnation must go forward. You are meant to incarnate in your lives the theme of your adoration. You are to be taken, consecrated, broken and distributed that you may be the means of Grace and vehicles of Eternal Charity'.

Clearly they must ask themselves how else could such a Body be formed and manifest itself in the life of the world today. The words imply something more closely knit together, more disciplined as to method, more purposeful in intention, more possessed of a common mind, more discriminating in its dealings with the world, than that loose aggregation of people that sits or kneels in the pews at times of services. If their coming together is restricted in time to a few hours in a week they must learn to economise time as one of their greatest gifts. Again and again in Péguy's poetry the temporal is acclaimed as that which the Eternal God has regarded 'and invested with His glory'. It is a note

but little heard in the greater part of church life today. A sense of
urgency is missing. Resources of time and attention are frittered
away.

Much has been said in recent years of the need of the Church
to 'dialogue with the world', with men of other faiths and with
those who profess no faith. This in turn may be traced to Buber's
lifelong work with its sustained appraisal of that which lies
between man and man and between man and God, an area of encounter charged with the possibilities of recognition and revelation, of turning towards or turning away in virtue of which
human life might blossom or wither. Dialogue itself springs from
and expresses an attitude quite different from that which was
represented by proclamation, sermon and lecture. The encyclical
Ecclesiam Suam spoke of prayer as dialogue, as part of the dialogue
of salvation begun by God with His people. It went on to
describe the use of it as something necessitated by the pluralism of
society in the modern world and by the maturity of men in their
social relationships. Some efforts were made to act upon such advice but it may be questioned whether many considered it to be a
gravely important matter or saw the issue as Péguy saw it in
terms of the decreation which must follow from men's inability
or unwillingness to speak with each other.

'An eternal foundation does not exclude the need to begin
anew.' The rebirth of the parish as an essential part both of
prayer and christianised life depends to a great extent upon such
groups as have been described being ready to see their task in the
first place as that of learning a new language, not a language
which they invent as the 'in-talk' of a closed circle but a language
already being spoken in various tongues throughout the world
and which they learn to translate for themselves. They must expect to be puzzled and perplexed as they strive to learn it and
quite dumbfounded by what it implies. 'The appearance of a new
language announces ... the coming into being of a new experience, a new self-understanding, a new vocation, and conse-
quently, a different man and community.' All that Rubem Alves
has described as 'the language of faith' now welling up in the
Latin-American world is relevant here. The groups must learn to

think of themselves not as 'study-groups', discussion-groups or prayer-circles but as communities of faith setting out like Abraham responding to God to find out for themselves what it means to be growing up to the full stature of the children of God at this time. They will study, discuss, break bread and pray together. They will try to act upon what they see. They will as surely keep contact with other groups of their kind on as wide a basis as possible. There is no reason why the smallest groups should not be open to concerns of a world-wide nature. It is their job to make personal matters of what otherwise will be treated as mere news or information. Through each of them must flow the insights and the strength of the whole Body of which they are part.

Speaking of the function of the *Cahiers* Péguy wrote, 'We have the meagre duty of keeping the communications between them open, of enlightening the ones about the others, of informing them about the others. We are charged, as though by chance, with making people communicate through us who do not want to communicate'. The parish is refounded when men take the trouble to set about doing this. It is not with much speaking that it will be done. Part of the task lies in disengaging men from a dead language current in Church and State. A faith or political commitment that is choked by dead metaphors, slogans and clichés however orthodox can have little part to play in the making of all things new. In Péguy's judgement the curés had lost the parishes because they had imposed such a language on their people, excluding from the sphere of religious devotion those things that were realities of their working lives, disparaging as profane what did not conform to their patterns of piety, thwarting the growth of a common speech that embraced their experience of life with gestures of christian faith. The outcome in terms of the spiritual life had been a disaster for both. A dumb laity made for an arrogant inwardly-fearful clergy, for a hollowness where communion should have reigned.

We are seeking no rejuvenation therefore of the parochial institutions of the past but the re-occupation of life now rapidly being de-Christianised by a new venture of faith both underpinned

by and expressive of prayer, a prayer that is finding itself as a
swimmer learns to swim in the medium of the world it enters.
The root stock of such praying is God's engagement of Himself
with the created world, with all its labours, pains and
achievements. The new language of prayer can be generated only
by a bold willingness to take hold of that world, to treat it in all
its details as a milieu divin. Péguy, who attached enormous importance to the founding of homes and families, farms and factories, cities and international relations, sought to have such
foundations laid in the field in which the spirit of Christ could
work upon them. Only so could they ever be richly creative in
turn. A comment made by a loader employed in the markets of
Paris years later makes clear what Péguy discerned. 'Right in the
heart of that reality, amid the crates and the roar of the crowd,
there are, it is true, two churches of stone. But the Church herself
is utterly absent. With the best will in the world I could not find
a trace of her, apart from a few distorted folk-memories . . .
Once one is immersed in this new life, nothing counts any more.
There must be a search for a new rhythm of prayer.'

Such foundations, Péguy believed, were already provided for
in Christ's work. The job of prayer lay in relating these necessary
human forms like family, parish and State to that work, recognising that change and continuity alike called for the work to be
done unceasingly if the true relationship were to be maintained.
It could only be true in virtue of new discovery. The world and
its relation to God had to be remade all over again day after day.
It was to that re-creative work that Péguy gave the name *Mystique*. We shall need to examine it more fully later for it entered
into all his thinking about human life and God's dealings with it.
Because creation proceeded afresh each day prayer must be a new
scanning of the scene with a readiness to discern what God was
about. Péguy's *Jubilate* is filled as much with what God is about
to do as with what He has done. It needed french eyes at times to
be really alive like that. In respect of the thing called the parish
the going was hard for as we have seen he believed that the clerks
had gone to infinite trouble to displace the *mystique* of Christ's
foundation and to substitute for it a false *mystique,* a *mystique* that

despised the world that God loved and brutally came to terms with a worldy idolatry, a *mystique* that dared to imagine that God had created the whole of His creation not only badly but pointlessly and emptily.

Nevertheless the pursuit of the true *mystique* must go on. The new rhythm of prayer in such a scene meant setting aside the substitutes offered and knowing why this had to be done. It meant a repeated effort to find where and how the new form of the parish or city could be laid hold of. Men would learn in setting about it to discover the way. 'One always knows the way,' wrote Péguy, 'I mean, there is always someone who knows it for one . . . We are entering into an unfamiliar land, an unknown land, an unknown land, a strange land, which is that of Joy. A hundred times stranger, a hundred times less known, a hundred times less us, than the kingdom of suffering, but a hundred times deeper and, I believe, a hundred times more fruitful'.

To pray the parish today for ourselves involves us then in this kind of task that Péguy discerned, in an unwearied probing and sifting of what is there, an honest rejection of what is unworthy of the common life in the Body of Christ to be found in its present forms, a courageous effort to build anew, an expectation that the help needed will be forthcoming, an ungrudging readiness to pay the cost, a stubborn and joyful hope that it will be done. It begins in the place where we are. Péguy, so often sick at heart and lonely, did not cease to believe that the springs of Grace would burst from the obdurate rock. His sense of the past confirmed it; his hope of the future expected it. There in the temporal foundations of the past 'like a farm in the Beauce, a house, a family or a dynasty, in cities of prayer like Cluny, Citeaux and Vézelay' were the signs to direct men forward.

In the *Cahier Notre Jeunesse*, Péguy broke out into one of those interminable sentences such as we find at the beginning of the Epistle to the Ephesians — how can a man stop when he has really begun to describe the action of God? — in praise of 'a french parish at the beginning of the fifteenth century, at a time when there were french parishes . . . in the days when there was Christendom, in an age when there were saints, at a time when there was such a thing as charity'. He was not sentimentalising his history but celebrating his conviction and putting it forward as we must as a declaration of intent. He understood that a new conception of the parish had got to be sought for a new foundation in faith to be attempted. *Mystique* did not produce blueprints or programmes. It looked for a child to nurture, it listened for a voice to be heard and answered. Its business was to perceive the judgement already passed upon things grown rotten and corrupt, to acknowledge dire need and to wait and hope for and respond to the signs of new life springing up. Christendom was gone. Quicker than most of his contemporaries to perceive the post-Christendom world, Péguy called men to look to the future. 'You shall call for a miracle, taking Christ at His Word' wrote Padraic Pearse as he himself yearned over Ireland's liberation. Men are no doubt too quick to decide what form that miracle should take. Péguy who called for it from the depths of his being was more willing to wait and to grow more expectant by waiting.

5. 'Mystique' and 'Politique'

'We cannot be in a closer relation to God than the one He Himself
provides by means of His own modest pressure upon us.'
                              Gregor Smith, *The New Man.*
'What if a man should succeed in laying his hand upon 'the chain of being' that runs through Nature and so become an interpreter of God?'
                              F. Meinecke, *Historism.*

Péguy is known to many by a single phrase: 'Everything begins
as a *mystique* and ends as a *politique*'. So far as they understand the
meaning he gave to those terms, they are possessed of a clue to his
life and work, not least to his prayer. But there are two
difficulties to be faced. The process of probing to which we have
already referred went on in all directions in Péguy's mind and his
repeated use of a word quite often covers a change of meaning.
The connotations multiplied as he used it. He was a poet explor-
ing a world by means of words. He was not a systematic thinker.
He could be unjust to himself, to others and to his own cause in
moods of truculence and indignation.

The second difficulty lies in the frequent misconstruction of
these terms by others. *Mystique* is related to mysticism, to a
mystical view of life, while *politique* is taken to mean politics used
in a disparaging way. So understood they leave the impression
that Péguy courted a vision that either stood in danger of being
soiled by contact with worldly affairs or could lend itself to
becoming the inspiration of a crude totalitarian system. Nothing,
I think, could have been further from the truth that Péguy sought
to honour.

A starting place must be sought elsewhere. The young Péguy
learning his Socialism from his blacksmith friend and from his

own experience of a working-class life reacted against the christian Church and was proud to ally himself with the damned of
the earth. Politics meant at that stage a part in the workers'
struggle to overthrow a corrupt and oppressive 'system and to
prepare the way for a new society. The Socialist movement in
France was gaining in strength, discovering leaders, enlarging its
theoretical understanding of its task. Péguy was wholly involved
in that. But this child of Orléans was also in mind hooked onto a
still wider theme or a still wider vision of what the cause was
about. In the opening words of *Le Mystère de la Charité de Jeanne
d'Arc* it is the word perdition – *la perdition* – damnation which
rings out in Joan's anguished lament. 'Et ce qui règne sur la face
de la terre, rien, rien, ce n'est rien que la perdition.' [1] In time we
are confronted with the demand Joan makes: 'How are they to be
saved?' Some years would pass before Péguy confessed himself to
be a christian but it is clear that from the outset it was human life
in terms of damnation and salvation that occupied his mind.
'How are they to be saved?' was to remain the great agitating
principle throughout his life.

It is difficult to use these words precisely, so charged have they
become with the overtones of revivalist meetings and the crude
fundamentalist pictures that have been used to convey their
meaning to other generations. It is no less difficult to use them in
a world that has 'put out the lights of Heaven' and 'dismissed
Hell with costs'. We may not be able to use them at all to engage
men's attention as we would wish unless we can learn to see them
in terms of the future and not of the past, in terms of life and not
of an 'after-life', in terms of God to be found ahead as the goal of
living and not of God described in the words of a byegone
world. A good deal of the shift in theological understanding in
our time has been in that direction, a good deal of the perplexity
of men and women in religion has arisen from having to turn
round and face the future when for centuries they had been accustomed to take their direction from the past. They have

1. 'And what reigns on the face of the earth, is nothing, nothing, nothing but perdition.'

repeated 'as it was in the beginning' too many times to take easily
to the change and it is understandable that in the process God
Himself seems often to be lost to sight.

Yet as we learn to make it we discover how things are made
new. Faith, hope and charity, so far from being dismissed, take
on a quite new significance and importance in human life. They
become the resources with which we approach the future.
Without them we can do nothing. The expectation that grace is
working ahead becomes a sober serious attitude. Truth issues a
challenge to men prepared to be explorers and their freedom is
seen to be requisite to their spiritual growth. All aspects of life
take on a new look. The Arts are accorded a prophetic function
and History enables man 'to rise to a consciousness of his own
historicity'. A new world is seen to be coming into existence, and
at that point salvation and damnation take on a profound importance.

It was with such a revolution that Péguy was fundamentally
concerned, thinking ahead of his time and perplexed by his own
insights. What did the salvation of the world really mean? He
would have echoed Emilia's words 'The world is a great place',
knowing quite well that men were accustomed to carving it up
into politics, religion, war and the like, trimming the pieces to
make them food for their gods and means for their own satisfaction. Who cared for the world? Salvation appeared to have
shrunk to concern for individual souls and for them the world
was of no concern save as an occasion of stumbling. The creation
could almost be thought of as a mistake. But Péguy was not to be
shaken. God loved the world and men's lives were not
detachable from it nor fragmented into self-chosen pieces. All the
diversities of the world must be contained in a unifying love
apart from which they must inevitably be lost. There was perdition, the grim possibility of such lostness. But there too was the
Word of salvation. It had entered the world and the world had
done what it could to eject it but the Word remained. Péguy was
not to be robbed of faith in that 'Christian operation'. It was
there in the world at work and the world was not to be understood rightly save in terms of its presence and mission. That

mission itself was utterly mistaken if men failed to see it poised on
the fate of a single human being for that was the measure of
salvation.

It followed that politics no less than any other human activity
stood in direct relation to this christian operation. Politics played
a considerable part in all worldly affairs. Political decisions
affected all aspects of life. Péguy saw the men of the Third
Republic deciding the fate of lives in Indo-China no less than
those of the children of France, and pursuing the policies they
adopted with no thought as to how these stood in relation to the
work of Christ. He was not in their world apparently, however
sharply a few voices like that of Péguy insisted He was. Not a
few people also professed to have no political interests but were
clearly moved by fears and prejudices of wholly political origin.
They subscribed to the world of the politicians without a question and Péguy was appalled. Such people were dismissing the
Christ from His world as if He had no business to be there.
Perhaps they were afraid of meeting Him there.

To Péguy thus concerned with the salvation of the world it
could not but be that the spiritual life and prayer must be concerned with all that went on in politics as in other aspects of life.
Politics meant so much. 'Politics is not merely the efficient and
just organisation of the community, so undertaken that human
life can proceed unhindered towards its self-realisation in other
spheres, nor is it, least of all, the efficient and just allotment,
regulation and exercise of power. Politics involves nothing less
than the common self-determination of mankind towards consciously chosen historical goals'. The field is one in which faith,
hope and charity are exercised in making choices, and in which
the right and duty of the servants of God to participate in them
must be accepted and performed.

From his earliest years Péguy took the political scene in a
serious fashion, and as he moved steadily towards a fuller
awareness of the christian operation, his sense of the cruciality of
political decision deepened . . . It gave him no rest in other men's
agreed positions and they soon suspected or rejected him. He was
well aware of the faith-destroying outcome of the dogmatism of

the party-line, whether in Church or State, and of the ease with which the relations of men in society could in the process of rapid economic change be dehumanised and subjected to merely manipulative policy. Contributing to the lostness of mankind they would be upheld as shrewd political gains. Péguy's political sensitivity fed into his prayer as the years went on the evidence of an increasing rejection of personal values, of a steady encroachment on the human aspect of the interests of power and wealth. He saw those communities which had nourished the growth of men towards a larger measure of freedom and responsible life subjected to persistent attack. His own response was sharp. His prayer became a militant act, a constant summoning up of spiritual vigilance to withstand and expose the threat of corruption and betrayal. 'The holy war is everywhere at once.' It involved both the Third Republic and the Church. In both he saw the displacement of the *mystique* of the christian operation by a *politique* assiduously served by men who both feared and hated the christianisation of the world, its total salvation in Christ.

Mystique meant nothing less than the conjunction of the spirit of God at work in the world with the activities of men in the founding and practice of their institutions. It was essentially active, the working of leaven in the meal. *Mystique* was the true response of men to the prompting and supporting of grace. It set them all in the dimension of God's creative-redemptive act. It honoured them to the extent that they embodied within themselves a faithful reply to the presence of Christ in their midst. Institutions of every kind would in the process of history come and go, providing for opportunities of ever new expressions of *mystique*.

Politique, on the other hand, set in as a process of dislocation, a rejection of that conjunction, a choosing to go it alone. It became an end in itself, ever seeking an aggrandisement of its own power, suspicious of and ready to suppress whatever challenged its own authority. *Politique* thus indulged became an idolatry, ready to generate its own false *mystique* to secure the devotion of men whom it pressed into its service. It represented a perversion of the authentic use of men's institutions, closing the horizons of human life and denying freedom to the critics lest its authority should be undermined. It made heresy the great sin and in so doing stultified language itself. It could not but function in a mechanical fashion, having no objective in time but its own continuance. Its servants were compelled to tamper with history to try to ensure that the image it now presented was seen to be without questionable antecedents.

Péguy came to see the great problem of his time in terms of a loss of *mystique,* the *mystique* of the Republic, of the Socialist cause, of christianised Europe, of man in the modern world. He believed it to be a time of crisis, of spiritual battle, in which he had a real part to play. 'The least of us is a soldier.' He did not foresee a time when fronts of various kinds, stormtroopers and commandos would appear throughout the world, but he felt the strain of the approaching conflict. He was to spend his life endeavouring to lay bare the true issues to be faced, knowing well the ease with which a false *mystique* could be employed to get men to fight the wrong battles. He himself could be often intemperate and harsh in his judgements of men but his faults were the outcome of a zeal for the *mystique* he fought for. He was not a profound or constructive political thinker and there were times when he appeared in the Belloc-Chesterton manner to invest some achievements of the past with a romantic splendour at the expense of historical judgement. 'He had no sense of proportion: the least obstacle was intolerable to him.' He was at his worst in dealing with academic foes, at his best in his analysis of the contemporary world and the place of the Christian Church within it and in pointing to the need for a new sense of *mystique* to give spiritual force and direction to political efforts in the modern world.

Two generations later we may well ask whether the Christian Church has, despite documents like *Pacem in Terris* and the beginnings of dialogue with Marxists in Europe and Latin America, paid sufficiently serious attention either to the critique which Péguy offered or to the theme of *mystique* of which he wrote. A step forward has quite often been followed by one if not two in a backward direction. A generous proposal of social objectives in matters of living standards, education, race-relations and social concern for the deprived has all too often been lost in a confusion as to means. A *mystique* of imaginative power sufficient to unite men within and across the cultural-political frontiers of the world and to energise a great movement of prayer has not been found. The rungs of the ladder at this juncture are anything but clear.

To see what this means we may look at the scene from yet other angles. In *The Ascent of Man,* Jacob Bronowski spoke of physics as 'the great collective work of art in the 20th century' in that it created the imagery needed to enable men to portray and speak about the underlying structure of the universe and the dynamic of its evolution. 'The human imagination working communally has produced no monuments to equal it, not the Pyramids, not the *Iliad,* not the ballads, not the cathedrals.' (We may still ask whether Chartres was not a more adequate imaging of medieval man's life than anything we have known since then.) Bronowski went on to say that even so the picture was always incomplete and to be used with great humility. St Thomas Aquinas had said as much in his day. The imagery used in the biological field by Teilhard de Chardin, however more limited in authority, has likewise offered something of great value to men endeavouring to speak to each other about their social problems in the contemporary world, about the future of man. He has pictured the fully conscious nations needed to secure the unity of mankind. Without the communication that such adequate imagery is needed to make possible, the state of mankind must resemble that of a boy-Faust with seemingly unlimited technological know-how and an adolescent ignorance of himself. What *politique* coarsely exploiting a false *mystique* can do in such circumstances has already been shown to the world in Hitler's Europe. The search for the needed *mystique* must therefore go on.

To Bronowski's comment I would want to attach some lines from a poem of Edwin Muir entitled *The Refugees.* This too supplies yet another necessary image to the picture, recalling one that belongs by tradition to the christian *mystique,* – the refugee Son of Man. To have elevated Him to princely thrones and altars at the expense of His homelessness is to have lost sight of something of profound importance in man's understanding of his own condition. Those who are unmindful of it eat and drink, buy and sell, marry and give in marriage, and are overtaken by the floods. The Bible could not be more explicit about their case. Bronowski introduced those refugee figures again and again into his work, not only because so many of them contributed so much to the Ascent of Man, but also because such men were amongst the significant figures of man's history. They were no new phenomenon in the spiritual journey, but in an age of *politique* were likely to be forgotten.

> A crack ran through our hearthstone long ago,
> And from the fissure we watched gently grow
> The tame domesticated danger,
> Yet lived in comfort in our haunted rooms.
> Till came the Stranger
> And the great and little dooms.

Since Muir wrote the lines, themselves part of his own *mystique,* we have seen the cracked hearthstone give place to the gas-ovens and the holocaust, seen the fissure widen to engulf the ignorant and the learned, the poor and the wealthy, the primitive and the cultured. We have it today in its more obvious forms equipped with Distant Early Warning devices. Whether we have faced it in terms of *la perdition* is another matter. Faced as never before in human history by the need to rethink on a global scale the social and political relations of mankind and to observe them more attentively not only across continents but in the narrower conditions of our factories and cities, it becomes plainer that the problem is spiritual. Such things present themselves as the raw material out of which a new *mystique* must be embodied. They are the primitive soil, 'la première argile, la première terre', [1] to which Péguy as poet was constantly moved to return. They hold promise enough of being fit clay for such enterprise only if the

1. 'the earth's first clay, the primal loam'.

mystique is powerful enough to release the spiritual energy needed for the task of providing in the approaching unification of mankind for the freedom of men to grow up as persons.

'A ladder of increasing complexity' is Bronowski's description of the movement of the evolutionary process. It is no less true of the ladder of devotion. It may well be that great multitudes of men and women have no great wish to exercise the freedom that John Stuart Mill was eager to give them or to be greatly concern-ed with their duties as citizens of a new world. The problem is as old as Moses. The hebrew answer was that it was to be solved not by Leadership or Law external to the personal lives of men but by the writing of a Law of Love in their hearts and by the nur-turing of personal relations in their society. Confronting them by a redemptive act of God, it required men to respond in faith in the working out of that embodied answer.

Hebrew spirituality rose to that task in declaring a bond un-iting this people with one God and Father of all who loved righteousness in the minutest details of daily life who desired mercy and pity to transform men's dealings with each other. Christian spirituality imaged the unity of that Godhead as plurality of Persons whose equality of dignity and mutuality of love presented themselves as the pattern upon which human life could and indeed must be shaped. However secularised that pattern and the demands which it makes upon men may be today – and the secularisation may well be an important aspect of its entry into human life – the Christian operation seen in a vastly widened way continues the age-long attempted answer to the problem. Today it must call into its resources not only those that ecclesiastical tradition has retained but what physics, politics, poetry and sociology and a host of other fields of insight may af-ford.

It is out of these that the new ladder of prayer is to be made. If today a great leap forward commensurate with that made in the scientific and technological spheres in the past hundred years remains to be attempted in the social and political world, it is as a spiritual exodus activity that it must be seen. 'The Word leads us not away from history, but to history and to responsible participation in history.' It was in that way that Péguy saw his work. The battlefields have shifted far and wide since he wrote, but what he can help us in now – 'now and England' – is in learning to see where the issues are raised.

It was Now and France with which Péguy began. The *affaire,* the trial, condemnation, degradation and committal to Devil's Island of Lieutenant Alfred Dreyfus, a young Jewish officer accused of selling military secrets to a foreign power, polarised french society and provided an outlet for the discontents and fears of masses of people. The conflict it engendered was kept at fever heat by the revision of the trial some five years later with its senseless verdict of 'guilty with extenuating circumstances'. It continued until the quashing of the sentence another five years later and the restoration of Dreyfus to the army. There is a sense in which the *affaire* continued until it involved all Europe. In the conflict the Third Republic was badly shaken. The Church was both deeply involved and bitterly attacked. The case of this unremarkable man went far to widen the cracks in a social-political structure for which few men had great respect.

That Péguy should have taken part in the struggle was natural enough. He followed and fought each stage of it with firm conviction and moral courage. Much more significant was his return to the matter in 1910 in the *Cahier Notre Jeunesse* with its sharp attack upon Halévy's essay on the *affaire* which he himself had published a few months before. The attack was in character in the sense that Halévy looked back on something concluded, Péguy on something of ever-continuing present importance. It is in his treatment of all such events as timelessly present that Péguy compels attention to their spiritual implications. This *Cahier* expressed more profoundly than ever before his conception of the holy war, of the christian operation, and of the extent to which he believed that Christianity in the modern world had been converted into the comfortable religion of the rich, 'everything, in fact, that is most contrary to its institution, to holiness, to poverty, to the Gospels'. Here also he spoke of himself as one among the last generation of those possessed of a republican *mystique,* as one 'charged with the task of informing people who have no wish to be informed'.

Péguy's *mystique* in the matter was declared with uncompromising force. The *affaire* had turned round the fate of a single man. 'What did we say? We said that a single injustice, a single crime ... is enough to breach the social compact, a single dishonour is enough to dishonour a people.' In this one man's case the risk of staking all had to be taken. 'C'est une gageure.' [1]One had to give up one's peace of mind for his sake. One had to learn from a single event that the spiritual health of a nation, of a Church, of a political regime, was at stake. Péguy the republican saw the Republic being drained of its *mystique* and converted into a thesis, (accepted or rejected, it doesn't really matter). Péguy the christian saw the christian Church no longer expressing the religion of the people but of a bourgeoisie, ('that is why the factory is still closed to the Church, and the Church to the factory'). Péguy the socialist saw the socialist movement with Jaurès at its head a victim to demagogy and the most shameless pursuit of political power, ('Our socialism was a religion of temporal salvation and nothing less').

He went on to contend that what mattered most was not the success of any political project so much as the continuance of the *mystique* from which it had sprung. *Mystique* was creative, *politique* a conjuring trick. What happened all too often was that men who were spiritually inert did not even notice that an action begun and truly aligned in a *mystique* was being converted into 'a derivative, parasitical, devouring *politique*'. Men were exposed to that peril because their praying did not alert them to the changing pressures of the society in which they lived and because a clerical *politique* diverted attention from them. Prayer which did not help men to discern the signs of the times had long ago been condemned by Christ. Péguy applied that test to himself with a deliberate care. Beneath the anger with which he attacked blind guides in both Church and State there was always at work a deeper purgation of spirit. His concern was with a political purity. He did not crave for a return to régimes of the past, the

---

1. 'It's a wager.'

monarchy of St. Louis or the republic of 1789, though he exulted in their *mystiques*. He recognised that all such embodiments of the interaction of the eternal and temporal were both incomplete and soon awry. All must give way to efforts at truer engagement. Prayer in the political world was that task accepted.

It has been said of Tillich that 'an important part of his greatness was his ability to endow with theological meaning the universal dissolution in two World Wars of the old certainties of european civilisation'. Péguy was no systematic theologian but a poet, and he did not live long enough to see for himself the breakdown in France and Europe of those civilised certainties. He nonetheless saw in his own experience the need of a man who would call himself christian to be alerted to that terrible prospect. Tillich indeed confessed, 'I am determined too much by the present *kairos*', sensing the danger that lay in too easy response to the currents of events, but in commenting on his words, Rollo May asked: 'on what level does he find his *kairos*? Does he penetrate to the depth where particular time is superseded, that level of the archetypes where the eternal myths of history such as Orestes and Oedipus have their existence, the depth where the future as well as the past finds its source.'

It was that effort to penetrate to the depths of every political question that constituted Péguy's work. 'The point of view we adopted was none other than the Eternal Salvation of France.' His political concern was inseparable from 'the dire dimension of the final thing'. As a christian he refused to believe in the final abandonment by God which damnation implied, but as a sensitive man he registered the pressures which were at the time shaping men to make choices which would carry them to such lengths. Kierkegaard had long since insisted that a man so placed could do no more than express the lostness of the time but Péguy was a more stubborn fighter and a more convinced believer in the stirrings of grace in the countryside of France. He found in Geneviève and Joan a depth that afforded him hope for the future. Clinging to that hope he went on celebrating his own strange joy in victory.

It was inevitable that he should put all the emphasis he could upon the question of human freedom. It is his *mystique* of freedom that makes him so relevant today. That concern expressed itself in at least three ways: in his poetry where freedom is constantly a great theme, in his political activities whether in support of workers or in his following of debates in the Chamber and conflicts in the Press, and finally in his bid for freedom in christian thought which anticipates much that has become a source of conflict in the post-Vatican II world.

'One can almost recognise a christian, a good christian', he said 'from the fact that he is tried with endless worries'. In his poetry which we shall consider in more detail later his worries were subordinated to an ebullient conviction that frenchmen knew better than anyone else in the world the importance of freedom. 'That is why, God says, we love these frenchmen so much, they have liberty in their blood all that they do, they do freely.' That freedom reflected the freedom of God Himself and was to be seen as 'the centre and heart and germ of my Creation'. Péguy repeated this over and over again in the *Mystery of the Holy Innocents*.

When we look at his political activities the source of the worries is more evident for he was engaged in a battle with the leaders of both Church and State. Put simply, the fight was on because these men were not interested in human freedom at all. The parliamentary parties conducted their own warfare for political advantage, translating all human affairs into political terms. 'As a result they understand nothing and prevent others from understanding anything.' It was the political converted into the sole end of man that roused Péguy to fury. As for the clerks of the Church they connived at the disaster by losing the people committed to their care and by totally misreading the problem of the modern world. They did not appear to realise that a de-christianised society, a world that had learned to do without Christianity, was already here and daily grew more contemptuous of a Church that appeared unwilling to address itself to its real task. The battles of both lay and clerical partisans evaded the great problems of poverty and injustice, of community and responsibility. Their invocations of republican or christian zeal were made only to lend sentimental force to the most hollow gestures. They made no real attempt to deal with a society which forced men to live for the sake of production, to produce for the sake of profits, to make profits for the continuance of the process in which the whole world and its resources would be shamelessly exploited. Abdicating their responsibility for the spiritual and moral problems thus created and for the misery inflicted upon the weakest members of society, the clerks contented themselves with a privatised version of christian faith which handed over a once christianised France to its sworn enemies. 'One and the same sterility withers the city and Christendom.'

It is in the contention Péguy made for the freedom of christian thought that his most significant contribution is made. What did Péguy understand by freedom? He had found his way to the christian faith in spite of the clerks and the church he believed in was not easily to be seen in the structure that the clerks so foolishly defended. The place of the christian was not there at all but elsewhere. As he wrote of Joan: 'She was like a soldier who fought not only on the boundaries, but whose own hearth and home had become an immense, universal boundary'. Freedom meant nothing less than a man's ability to choose those frontiers for himself.

Tillich in describing his own life in the book entitled *On the Boundary* has made clearer in our own day what Péguy understood by fighting on the frontiers. 'The concept of the boundary might be a fitting symbol', Tillich wrote 'for the whole of my personal and intellectual development'. Development was not a word that Péguy would have used to describe his own journeying but he was well aware that 'the boundary is the best place for acquiring knowledge', and for the exercise of faith and hope. Still more he saw it in temporal terms as the moment of engagement with 'the secret event', the profound inward operation which sprang from Christ's going ahead in His world. Freedom meant the ability and willingness of a man to leave behind all the forms and structures of the past, to make the bet of faith, to risk encounter with chaos, to leap over the walls which offered protection, and to live without the certainties of the past.

Prayer was in truth the continual re-committal of a man to that migrant life.

We should lose the real force of Péguy's demand if we lost sight of or forgot his immense valuation of the products of time. The founding of cities, of families and of cultures was for him a serious, sacred act, having its place in the whole creative combined operation of God and man. He loved the productions of time. But to set them between mankind and the future, to convert them into defences against further change, was to obstruct the Spirit itself, to attempt to ward off the pressures which God exerted upon His people.

If one asked where those pressures were being made in the social-political life of the world he was ready to point to the conditions of poverty, disease, oppression and exploitation which were evident if men cared to look. 'See that thou deal thy bread to the hungry, that thou let the oppressed go free.' Christians must take their place not as spectators but as participants in the relief and release of the needy and enslaved. Wherever the poorest man was compelled to suffer injustice, it was the job of the christian to act as the prophet Nathan did and not cease to convict the unjust of their sin. 'You see what Christianity is like. You have taken the simplest of all values, all the human values and made them divine. You take everything to God, everything back to God. You touch God on all sides.' Nor was it a matter for the paternalism that so often had been used to compromise in such things. Human dignity and freedom demanded a willingness to listen, to treat with the 'whole person' with whom one was confronted, to admit that there could be room for a diversity of solutions to the problems of human liberation, and that it was the business of spirituality to pay attention to them. Not to be involved was to deny the Christ already there. 'Of all the bad uses which can be made of prayer and the sacraments' wrote Péguy, 'none is so odious as an idleness which does not work or act, and afterwards, and during, and before, asks that prayer should make up the difference'.

We have come far since Péguy in the name of christian *mystique* challenged the resort to *politique* by men too faithless or too selfish to commit themselves to the christian operation. Not a few of the concepts like dialogue and liberation and the actual involvement of many christians in the work and politics of the world have their roots in the things over which he brooded and prayed. A theology of hope has become a recognised feature of our time. A willingness to admit that it is the totality of mankind that is the field of the Spirit's work has begun to reshape the attitude of the Churches towards their own styles of life and work. When Péguy spoke of the catholic renaissance that was coming about through himself it was no boastful expression of self-importance, but a glad cry of recognition that the saving operation at work in the world was there to be felt and known and expressed each day of his life. Born in a bleak age he nevertheless knew in his flesh the stirrings of Spring and saluted with joy 'a childhood, a burgeoning, a promise, an engagement, an attempt, an origin, a beginning of a Redeemer, a hope of salvation, a hope of redemption'.

6. The Communion the Saints

'In the course of conversation someone remarked, "There are no saints nowadays". Father Coutourier answered rather gruffly, "Madame, Saint Catherine of Siena's mother used to say, 'There are no more saints' "'.'

Julian Green, *Diaries.*

On the backs of the dead,
See, I am borne, on lost errands led,
By spent harvests nourished.

Edwin Muir, *The Debtor.*

'I could go on writing of Jeanne d'Arc for twenty years' said Péguy, and so, of course he did, not writing works of erudite scholarship about her, but in a very personal way conversing with her, observing her intently, praying with her, entering into her anguish and her hopes, always learning from her. She was, allowing for all the differences of outlook and circumstance, the Beatrice to his Dante. She belonged to the french countryside, to his birthplace Orléans, and to the great Loire itself:

Et c'est le souvenir qu'a laissé sur ces bords
Une enfant qui menait son cheval vers le fleuve. [1]

He had no doubt that the trumpets sounded for her on the other side of another stream into which she had gone down with equal courage. Alone yet not alone, she belonged to the great community of the saints of God, and was glorious not only for what she was and did by the grace of God, but also in her represen-

1. 'For on that river's banks remains the memory
   Of a child who guided her horse towards the stream.'

tative role. To his profound sense of the solidarity of God's people she gave the especial joy of personal recognition. They understood each other. Peasant and christian they stood together. There was in him a great readiness to recognise the anonymity of that multitude which no man could number. In what was to prove almost his last piece of work he wrote: 'Man turns back to his race and immediately behind his mother and father he sees four more abreast, and immediately after, immediately behind he sees nothing. Why not say so, he is proud to plunge into this anonymity'. The great number were as though they had never been. The brief continuance of a name in the mouths of men meant very little. What really mattered, what gave joy to a man, was that out of this unnameable throng a glance, a gesture, a word could by the mercy of God establish a bond of a personal kind, intense and real in this present life and a promise of something greater to be disclosed. With Joan, this lonely man, Charles Péguy, deeply conscious of sins and out of communion with the Church of his day, knew himself to be in communion with the people of God and with Christ their head.

Such indeed is the meaning of the communion of the Saints, a fragment of Christian truth too much neglected perhaps today. The more truly we come to understand personal life the more we are learning to see ourselves not standing apart from others but bone of their bone, flesh of their flesh, spirit of their spirit. We are what we share. This communion of saints means also that the enmeshment of our lives is not in some neutral colourless fabric but in an achievement already resplendent with glory to God.

Few men immediately and wholeheartedly involved in the work and warfare of the world can have been more joyfully conscious of communion with the saints than Péguy. His awareness of Joan was a great tap-root which nourished all that he lived for and focussed all that his imagination grasped, so that as we try to understand him and in turn seek help from him, we have to look at the part she played in his life. 'What we need, God, what we finally need, is a woman who would also be a saint.' That was the expectation that he nursed in his own silent supplication. But Joan was not to be thought of alone or apart from the great company of saints, especially those of the french countryside whose presence as we said earlier added the personal element to the holy ground of France. They, St. Aignan, St. Martin, St. Eloi, St. Geneviève, St Rémi, St. Ouen, to name only a few, were immediately distinguishable members of the family: 'one is in communion with them'. St. Michael and St. Catherine and the Blessed Virgin herself played no less a part in the shaping of men's lives. Halévy has left a brief vivid picture of the Péguy household as he visited it one day, 'a wash-day going on in the open air, Péguy himself playing with the children and everyone chattering about St. Catherine as if she had only gone out ten minutes ago'.

It is possible to see this as a quaint revelation of an unwordly streak in Péguy's mind, a survival of outlook from the Ages of Faith before parsons left off conjuring and fairies dancing, an illustration of the sweet seriousness of a child telling a fanciful story and no more. But Péguy was not unworldly nor fanciful nor out of date. His whole life like that of Kierkegaard was consumed with a passion for the truth in religion, in politics, in poetry, a life of unremitting warfare which burned out the inessentials and etched deeply the things he lived by.

To understand him at all we have to see both the likeness and unlikeness he bears to Kierkegaard. 'From the beginning of Christianity' wrote Theodor Haecker, 'there have always been men whose mission it was to separate the divine from the human, the heavenly from the earthly, and faith from philosophy, with all the sharpness of paradox and passion; and then again others whose mission it was after the air had been cleared by storms and by these separations, to restore harmony and peace once more'. Kierkegaard belonged to the first type, Péguy to the second, though the peace-making was no less strenuous than the disruption. Péguy did not blur the lines of the divine and human when he insisted on their engagement. He could not have afforded confusion of the two any more than a precision-instrument maker could afford inaccuracies. The truth of the christian Gospel would lose its entire significance if the twain that met in the Christ were not twain at all but vaguely related the one to the other. Whatever partition there was between things human and divine He had broken down 'so making peace' but stupendous mystery it remained, known only to those who likewise engaged themselves in it. The saints were evidence that the conjunction held.

From the outset then as we try to see what the communion of the saints meant in practice to him, it is important to follow as closely as we can Péguy's own reflections on it. Like Eliot's Thomas of Canterbury he would have affirmed that martyrs were not made by accident; they had their necessary place in the divine ordering of history. He knew no less that saints were not men and women of special merit or demi-gods set between heaven and earth. They were soldiers rather, selected for a particular job, proved warriors in the field, and therefore able to help all those who came into the struggle later. To pray was to participate in their work, their suffering and their joy. Péguy, always a soldier at heart, saw himself drafted into such ranks, not claiming a title for himself, but exultant at being there, impatient like Joan in her youth to prove his fidelity, being seasoned like Madame Gervaise to accept the drudgery it entailed. Always it is from the heart of this enlistment that he prays. 'We must pray for ourselves in others, among others, in the communion of all.' Against the anguish he experienced in his own solitary battles for the truth, he pitted the great 'block of holiness' which the saints made up, rejoicing that 'in the folds of their cloaks they bore the glory of God and the body of Jesus'.

All this rests on the conviction that God so loved and loves these children of His that He pours out upon them the rich diversity of His grace. In the limitations and the achievements of their lives they spell out for us what it means to be truly human. They fight their many battles generation after generation with the resources that seem so pitiful yet prove to be in use indicative of a human fulfilment beyond all dreams. They are plainly imperfect creatures, they are often defeated and they recover, they deny Him and they repent, they choke and splutter like a child who is learning to swim – an image very dear to Péguy – and the Father Himself will marvel at the triumphant use they make of His gifts. Saints are exclamations of delight, the delight of both God and man. What is more worth marvelling at than that the Glory of God should be so revealed in His creatures? That matter and circumstance compounded into a frail human life should not be, in Teilhard de Chardin's words 'just the weight that drags us down, the mire that sucks us in, the bramble that bars our way . . . but our accomplice towards heightened being'? It was said of Rabbi Aha, a contemporary of the Emperor Julian, that when he died the stars shone by day. Saints are the promise that the image of God is not effaced from the human clay that was created to bear it but that His likeness is being perfected in us. The communion of the saints is witness to the many-sidedness of that image being translated into reality in the lives of men.

This step upon the ladder of prayer is rich in the materials assembled in history and waiting to be used. Our task is one of construction, of learning to reflect on lives so lived that they help us to handle our own. Silence is needed to permit us to distinguish their features. In an essay on protestant mystics, W. H. Auden pleaded for such attention, quoting words of Sir William Osler, 'Half of us are blind, few of us feel, and we are all deaf'. He went on to urge that we should most fervently pray for gifts of hearing and sensibility, that we might translate into our own tongue the witness made by the saints. Saints are part of the language of humanity in its dialogue with God, the moments of conversation that kindle towards understanding, the evidence that the language of prayer is not an algebra to be mastered and skilfully put to use but a relation to be entered into. To grow up unaware of them, to be ignorant of their diversity of speech, must mean a kind of spiritual disinheritance, a human diminishment, a narrowing of our capacity to communicate.

It is reported that recommendations to cut down the saints' days of the anglican calendar are being made. Observance of them has not been one of the most outstanding features of our time. What matters more than the number of days commended for such use is more fundamental recognition in Péguy's sense of what we understand by our communion with the saints. Our failure, one suspects, is largely due to that over-individualisation that has so often set them apart like the bright scholars in a competitive world instead of bringing them nearer to us.

Péguy's attention to the saints was like the repetitive element in his poetry, a turning over and over of the speech that they embodied within themselves, so that no scrap of infinitely precious meaning should be lost. He rejected entirely the notion that they were 'there to inspire us', to be copies of virtue, to be set beyond human reach. He would have understood readily what Brémond meant in his words: 'In the measure that popular worship lifts them high above our criticism and clothes them with the whole uniform of attributes common to their class, the saving influence that flows from a living human individuality is at an end'. We have to dig deeper to make real use of the saints.

Péguy's conception of the communion of the saints carries us to the heart of his understanding of creativity. The poet, the maker in him, was fascinated by it. Creation and decreation were constantly in his mind. He thought deeply about the spiritual organism being shaped in human history, the Body whose head was Christ. Language became both the instrument and symbol of the consciousness of the Body, the Word taking flesh. As a poet he perceived that in it the mystery of Creation was re-presented anew. What he groped his way forward to understand was what George Steiner has illustrated for us in speaking of the grammar of the Hebrew prophets like Isaiah as 'enacting a profound metaphysical scandal – the enforcement of the future tense, the extension of language over time', and suggesting further that 'Shakespeare at times seems to "hear" inside a word or phrase the history of its future echoes'. Prophet and poet are alike responding to the living speech of a living God. Péguy the poet seems almost unwilling at times to move on from some word lest he should fail to hear in it the timely and timeless things it conveys. The mystical dialectic of the mount of Transfiguration is continued age after age and becomes the means by which mankind is freed from cycles of meaningless events. If such hugely momentous power is attached to words, what must be the worth of the silence they pre-empt? Saints were the people like Joan who listened and heard the voices.

What follows from Péguy's understanding of the communion

of the saints is a full sense of what we must for a moment call sacred history, though his own use of the word *mystère* to describe his longer poems was nearer the point. Sacred history has suffered much since the growth of 'secularised history' whose impact upon the outlook and faith of christians in the last two hundred years has been discussed in detail by Dr. Owen Chadwick in *The Secularisation of the European Mind in the 19th Century*. It was to be expected that frenchmen would play a great part in that work. Michelet, Taine and Renan indeed affected it more than others. Renan's *Life of Jesus* was perhaps the most influential book in the shaping of popular attitude towards religion that appeared. 'Meditations of piety' observes Dr. Chadwick, 'took Jesus out of history. Renan put him back into history', giving men a Christ they could understand. Both Taine and Renan attached a cultural civilising value to religion while Renan did all he could to describe a Jesus of great moral beauty for the multitude who wanted such a figure.

Péguy came into the fray in a *Cahier* in 1904 in an essay on history and the abuse of historical method entitled *Zangwill* when he himself was but finding his way to faith. What was it he attacked? Much as he prized the sharp probing critical spirit that God had given to frenchmen, Péguy was in search of something more. Sacred history meant more than perceiving events, establishing facts, laying bare motives and even interpreting all these things in terms of ideas and cultural movements. Péguy saw the professors of such historical method becoming the militant defenders of an authoritarian political world, foreclosing on the freedom of the spirit and imposing their own systems of thought as the reality of human life. Sacred history by contrast gave room for spiritual growth. The hebrew conception of it was heavy with responsibility. It laid upon men, as Pannenberg was later to say, 'the conscious burden of their own historicity' but the task was neither inhumanly heavy nor dehumanising. God who acted within it by grace, as we have seen already declared in Péguy's verse, wanted man to win.

Sacred history so understood is anything but the ecclesiastical in-talk that so often has been set over against the secular history of the day. What Péguy looked for, what indeed so much of his spiritual reflection turns on, is an image of the game with grace which could take the place once held in men's minds by the City of God and Christendom. The passing of the forms in which men had believed in these things was not to be lamented. What was important was the founding of a new version of the Holy City to take their place. Their disappearance had left men with little but the clipped fore-shortened notion of human life which secular history gave. Péguy surmised that Renan knew this and endeavoured in his own *defroqué* fashion to do battle against it. He also saw that something which had been fundamental to hebrew spirituality and which christians had learned to extend into their own world-view was rapidly disappearing. The Old Testament which the Church had insisted upon binding together with the New was becoming an unknown book. Something which had once sustained the poorest of God's people was being drained away. Men no longer counted upon the hidden grace and like the saints found room for it.

There is hardly a more lively description of it, couched in the tones of gentle mockery than a passage from Heine which Matthew Arnold quoted in his essay on that poet.

'There lives at Hamburg, in a one-roomed lodging in the Baker's Broad Walk, a man whose name is Moses Lump; all the week he goes about in wind and rain, with his pack on his back, to earn a few shillings; but when on Friday evening he comes home, he finds the candlestick with seven candles lighted, and the table covered with a fair white cloth, and he puts away from him his pack and his cares and he sits down to table with his squinting wife and yet more squinting daughter, and eats fish with them, fish which has been dressed in beautiful white garlic sauce, sings therewith the grandest psalms of King David, rejoices with his whole heart over the deliverance of the children of Israel out of Egypt, rejoices too that all the wicked ones who have done the children of Israel hurt, have ended by taking themselves off; that King

Pharaoh, Nebuchadnezzar, Haman, Antiochus, Titus, and all such people, are well dead, while he, Moses Lump, is alive and eating fish with his wife and daughter.'

The mockery is precise but we read the passage today with something a deeper intonation. Beneath the grotesque external features which men extended even to death in the extinction camps there lay a sustaining conviction that gave dignity and hope to generations of mankind. 'Next year in Jerusalem.' Sacred history means much more than the survival of the Chosen People or the progress of the missionary enterprise of the Church. It means the disclosure, generation after generation of the presence of the saints, of that interpenetration of things human and divine which Péguy described in the imagery of mortice and tenon, of the appearance among men and women of an interiority giving to personal life a capacity to be other than self-centred, of the energising of that life by an all-embracing love. Sacred history is, as I have already suggested, wedded to sacred geography, tradition to holy ground, in order that the presence should be located as firmly as possible in time and place, not as a journey's end but as a starting place. When T. S. Eliot writes of Little Gidding in these terms or the more casual visitor of Philip Larkin's poem *Church Going* speaks of

'A serious house on serious earth (it is)
In whose blent air all our compulsions meet,
Are recognised, and robed as destinies.'

we are confronted by recognition of intimations of transcendence which in Péguy's experience were the evidence of the communion of the saints.

Sacred history provided its own rungs for the ladder of prayer. 'One never prays apart from anyone ... that would be praying outside the communion.' It was manifestly the function of the saints to assure the man or woman who prayed at some moment of crisis, questioning, strain or joy that they were not alone and that what now appeared to them as an insupportable, meaningless or incommunicable matter could be seen in terms of necessary fulfilment. 'They were talking with Him of the decease which He must shortly accomplish in Jerusalem.' It is the business of the moments of transfiguration to reveal what the limitations of our ordinary experience hide from us, that both the personal struggles whose loss or victory threatens to be swallowed up in meaninglessness and the pure joy which ever and again breaks into our life, have their place in a much wider context and a meaning which is unassailable in time.

Péguy loved military manoeuvres. He looked upon the saints as picked soldiers posted, often unknown to themselves, to important positions, each with some special assignment to honour, each trusted to do what was needed. 'Sainte Geneviève, Saint Aignan, Saint Loup were not afraid of meeting heathen armies . . . And Saint Martin was a soldier. And Saint Bernard who preached the second crusade . . . In the folds of their cloaks they bore the glory of God and the body of Jesus.' But as Péguy knew, and as the great debate between Joan and Madame Gervaise in his poem makes clear the problem was to know one's assignment. The contradictions were inescapable. With the sharp remorselessness of a child Joan presses home the denial of Peter and obstinately maintains that frenchmen, men of the breed of Charlemagne, Saint Denis, St. Louis, would never have renounced the Christ. Madame Gervaise retorts that Joan is bringing division into the Church, setting some saints against others, bringing debate into the communion. 'There is only one race of saints which is the eternal race.' Yet Joan persists, driving home her point, 'You, Madame Gervaise, you would not have renounced Him', and adding her own determination not to do so. 'And the cock crew.' Madame Gervaise has no difficulty in replying, 'They are always talking about that cock . . . Alas, alas, there is not a cock in a farm that has not crowed over, that has not sounded, that has not heralded forth the rising sun, that has not recorded, every day, at each sunrise, worse denials . . . A cock crew for Peter; how many cocks crow for us: the breed is not extinct.' So the denials go on but that is not the last word. 'Jesus

forgave, and instantly, in advance, he had forgiven Peter's denial
... God send that God has acquired the habit.'

So the two aspects of Péguy's own nature find expression. The
battleground shifts from age to age, the contradictions remain.
The more men must take into their own hands the shaping of life
on the earth and the shaping of themselves, the more acutely are
they confronted with contradictions that remain. 'You offer God
what you have. You offer God what you can.' The offering is
always incomplete, the doing is always smirched with something
less pure than the occasion warrants. You see for yourself that
neither your own nor the efforts of all the saints can be extricated
from the sin that attaches to human action. At that point comes
the great test which Joan puts to her self, to Madame Gervaise, to
all human beings whatever. 'And when you see that your prayers
are in vain, what then?'

Péguy came to that point as all of us must again and again
throughout life. In his own comparatively short life he faced the
problems that a thoroughgoing involvement in politics at the
time laid on him. It was a continuing bitter experience. Today
we might well regard that time as innocent of the far vaster
problems that our own world now discerns. The range and scope
of human purpose has grown in almost infinite size and complexity, the pace of confrontation quickened. The situation can hardly be other than that in which men see themselves now possessed
of a power to shape human life as never before, now appalled by
the monstrous dimensions of the problem they have thus created
for themselves. The cynical, the timid, the worldlywise, the
wounded, are moved to join forces to declare that any change
must be for the worse. Acquiescence in oppression of mind and
body becomes an inviting option. Dostoievsky's Grand Inquisitor
takes on the look of a most efficient social worker. 'When your
prayers are in vain, what then?'

Not easily then but with a profound sense of suffering and
human dereliction Péguy answered through Madame Gervaise
'We know that a prayer is never in vain'. The answer was made
with a full knowledge of the brutal contradictions lying in wait
for those who made it, with a sharp awareness of the fact that the

saints had had to face such things. To celebrate St. Geneviève one
had to move on from the contemplation of the shepherd girl with
her sheep, the inviting stuff of pastoral poetry all down the years,
to cities in flames and men's bodies torn to pieces.

> Comme Dieu ne fait rien que par miséricordes,
> Il fallut qu'elle vît le royaume en lambeaux,
> Et sa filleule ville embrasée aux flambeaux,
> Et ravagée aux mains des plus sinistres hordes. [1]

One had to foresee not only cities in flames but the bodies of
the saints themselves, and to hear ahead of time the mockery of
those who would cry 'Where's your Good Old Cause now?' To
talk of a partnership in human history was inspiring indeed and
Péguy who loved creativity could not but rejoice in that. What
stretched the soul on the rack of this tough world was the hideous
truth that the partnership could be betrayed and that men could
find their pleasure in destruction. To see the french countryside as
Péguy did through eyes that noted the avenues of tall poplars
marking the road to some splendid chateau as a picture of Old
Testament prophets pointing their witness to Christ was solidly
reassuring. What haunted the mind was the knowledge that men
could ravage such things in the name of Christ Himself. Did
prayer remain valid when the centuries added new chapters to
that discernment?

Péguy's attachment to the communion of the saints was no
spiritual luxury. It was rather an extension into the total history
of mankind of his basic faith in God, of a faith tried to the utter-
most yet doggedly maintained. It is his assertion that 'I am not
alone', an act of faith that sprang from that which he placed in
God. Franz Rosenzweig had once described it in a letter: 'None
of us has solid ground under his feet; each of us is only held up by
the next man, and often, indeed most of the time (quite naturally,

---

1. 'Yet, since in but mercy only does God act
   She needs must see the kingdom torn to shreds,
   Her god-child city going up in flames,
   And ravaged by the hands of grim invaders.'

since we are neighbours mutually) hold each other up mutually. All this mutual upholding (a physical impossibility) becomes possible only because the great hand from above supports all these holding hands by their wrists. It is this, and not some non-existent "solid ground under one's feet" that enables all the human hands to hold and to help'. The upholding was an act of love as humanly 'natural' as that of the father supporting his son as he learned to swim, but the humanness had no meaning apart from the great hand of God. The saints were needed in every generation to make explicit to men that the fire refined but did not destroy the faith of christians. Péguy's concern was with the depth of human suffering that such calling involved; suffering as the 'highest form of action, a divinely potent means of satisfaction, recovery, and enlargement for the soul, – the soul with its mysteriously great consciousness of pettiness and sin, and its immense capacity for joy in self-donation'. Péguy approached the saints as a man seeking to learn from them the reality of the relationship which God had determined for them. He stayed with them to grasp the full truth of their re-creation. God says:

'There must have been some secret understanding between our Frenchmen and young Hope.

They are so marvellously good at it.'

7. Poetry and Prayer

'We only hear a tone once, only see a colour once, see, hear, touch, taste and smell everything but once, the first time. All life is an echo of our first sensations.'

Herbert Read, *The Innocent Eye.*

'There is a moment at which things come truly alive: the moment at which they are caught in all their subtlety by the imagination. Then they take to themselves meaning.'

A. Alvarez, *The Shaping Spirit.*

It has been said that modern times begin when man confronts his isolation, when he becomes aware of the break-up and disappearance of the various ties and bonds which once related him to God, to his fellows and to the earth. It is the dread discovery that 'we mortal millions live alone', the shudder that acknowledges the silence of the dark empty space, the moment of 'panic and emptiness' that overtakes the mind. Poets and novelists and playwrights have expressed it very fully. A great cultural epoch in which at one time men sang to celebrate the honour of the Gods, to justify God's ways to man, to affirm the rightness of the world because God was in His heaven, would appear to have come to an end. It did not, it does not, come easily or unchallenged. Baroque poetry, painting, sculpture have been described as a great imaginative effort on the part of men aware of the weakening hold of what once had been divine reality to 'keep open the avenues of communication between man and God'. Victorian England, too sober to indulge in such flights, had its own strenuous gestures to make, touching naturally enough the ladder or staircase once so plain:

I falter where I firmly trod.
And falling with my weight of cares
Upon the great world's altar-stairs
That slope thro' darkness up to God.

It is at this point that we look again at Péguy. Is he no more
than a belated straggler limping after a vanishing column, a voice
from a world now dead, a quaint survival of the 'mad' band of
singers whose inspiration came, it was alleged, from another
world? Or is he a portent of something quite other, a man who
breaks new ground, a poet whose imaginative power is able to
marshall words to speak not of a dead past but of timeless things
that break into our life today? Without trying to make him out
to be one of the world's major poets, may we see him as the
singer of what modern man most sorely needs, of a new sense of
relatedness, of communion, of meaning, of new vision of God?
He is by any standards an unusual poet, a man who came later
rather than earlier than others to being a poet at all. I believe him
to be not just 'the eccentric of french literature' and certainly not
a singer of a christian enclave in the modern world, but a serious
christian poet who points forward to a new understanding of
man's life in the world.

It is a pity that there was no Matthew Arnold to write an essay
on Charles Péguy but one can almost imagine what it would
have been like. One hears the author of the study of Joubert saying, 'One should be fearful of being wrong in poetry when one
thinks differently from the poets, and in religion when one thinks
differently from the saints', and again, 'because he sincerely loved
light, and did not prefer to it any little private darkness of his
own, he found light; his eye was single, and therefore his whole
body was full of light'. One notes the comment that Keats had
flint and iron in him, that Shelley's poetry was not 'entirely sane',
that the moment he reflected Byron was a child. One would hear
again the sharp description of english provinciality compared
with the broad stream of european culture, the demand for
'natural magic' and 'moral profundity' in poetry, and revel in the
juxtaposition of the works of the feeble protestant forces with the

collection of the Abbé Migne: 'How are they dwarfed by the catholic Leviathan, their neighbour. Majestic in its blue and gold unity, this fills shelf after shelf and compartment after compartment, its right mounting up into heaven among the white folios of the *acta sanctorum,* its left plunging down into hell among the yellow ocatavos of the Law Digest ... like one of the great Middle-Age cathedrals, it is in itself a study of life'. One would end in that naughtiest scene of all, 'a great room in one of our dismal provincial towns; dusty air and jaded afternoon daylight, benches full of men with bald heads and women in spectacles; an orator lifting up his face from a manuscript written within and without to declaim those lines of Wordsworth; and in the soul of any poor child of nature who may have wandered in thither, an unutterable sense of lamentation, and mourning and woe'. Péguy would, I think, have emerged, not entirely unscathed, but tested, tried and approved.

The business of poets is with words, with the power of language to articulate those things that lie at the roots of human life, to create the worlds in which men live, to incite us, to use Valéry's phrase 'to become rather than to understand'. It has been said that a poet may take flight from a single word, that he may hear in its uses and meanings both ancestral voices and tones of the years to come, that he may so conjure with it as to set free its locked-up ambiguities and awaken in men's minds a new intensity of living. Péguy's use of *jaillir*[1] and *jaillissement* is such a case:

'Car merveille c'est de cette eau même qu'ils font jaillir la source.'[2] There is ejaculation in a myriad forms; the upward thrust of sap, the fountains overflowing, the quickened pressure of the germ, the steady silent growth of trees, and the passionate leap of courage that the human spirit makes. Péguy's work is itself such a *jaillissement,* an irrepressible exuberance attended by many disconcerting features, but ordered by strong imaginative power. There is at all times a spiritual audacity in his work. He does not falter on the stairs, for having known the depths of misery he hurls himself upwards yet again.

1. 'jaillir' – to spring out or gush.
2. 'Wonder, that from this water indeed they make the spring to flow.'

To find titles descriptive of his way of writing, Péguy used two words to characterise his poems. Both illustrate the inclination of his mind, the kind of work he set out to do, the 'inscape' that was his vision. Both have a great bearing upon prayer. One of these was *tapisserie*, the other *mystère*. We have the *Tapisserie de Ste Geneviève* and the *Tapisserie de Notre Dame*: the *Mystère de la Charité de Jeanne d'Arc*, the *Mystère de la Porche de la Deuxième Vertu*, the *Mystère des Saints-Innocents* and a vast poem *Eve* which combines the qualities of both *tapisserie* and *mystère*. Both forms express in great detail Péguy's concern with the created order, his amazement and delight in its diversity, his refusal to grow indifferent to it, his perception of the Christ as the living Word by whom and for whom it exists. 'God has exploded in His creation', said Péguy, a whole generation before men had grown used to hearing of exploding stars and the primal explosion of the universe. This *jaillissement* of God is the counterpart of the 'energy' of William Blake, the source of eternal delight. It runs through all things and gives to his poetry a dynamic that prayer must use.

> What matters
> Is that we should move. Be always moving
> This is what counts, this, and how we move.

To say that Péguy retained the innocent eye of childhood would not strictly be true. He rediscovered it rather time after time because he was always ready to move – *suivre les indications* –, because he was ready to go back to the beginnings again and again without sense of loss, and to start at deeper levels of perception.

> It is true that we go over
> The same road twenty times,
> But in the sight of Divine Wisdom
> Everything is new.

As a consequence 'my little hope'

who wakes every morning and gets up
and says her prayers with new attention.

makes each day a new day in which it is possible 'to see your self
in your father's palace; and look upon the skies and the earth and
the air, as celestial joys,' exactly as Traherne filled rapturous
pages in saying. It is notoriously easy to grow sentimental over
childhood. Péguy escaped that snare though he wrote
voluminously about childhood, because his was not a backward
glance. It was always a starting again.

'Tapestry is a bright dream indeed' exclaimed William Morris
when he discovered for himself the glorious possibilities that
weaving held out for him. Craftsman of the same serious stamp as
Péguy, Morris possessed a far wider range of artistic gifts, a
greater talent for narrative verse, a keener eye for natural beauty,
a stronger sense of colour, (he said that Shelley had no eyes) than
the frenchman. Péguy on the other hand instinctively knew the
culture of catholic Christendom as one in whose veins it lived,
whereas for Morris it was something to be gleaned from literary
and artistic sources, and remained in the end an idealised world.
Péguy knew also the depths of spiritual conflict not just in
himself but through his own participation in the world in a way
unknown to Morris.

Both men even so saw tapestry, whether in wools or words, as
the right form and medium for much of the work they wanted to
do. The 'Earthly Paradise' is such a *tapisserie*. It aimed at weaving
together these stories and legends which expressed most fully in
Morris's judgment the truest perceptions of beauty that the dis-
tinctive cultures of the Western World had produced. Péguy
would not have rejected any of these. Into his own *paradis* he was
ready and anxious to pour all the working achievements of
mankind from the ploughshare to the cathedral. His tapestry
however has a more explicit christian design. Its theological
dimensions are firmer. Whatever episode it treats of has its place
in the unfolding story of the Word made flesh. It reaches back to
the creation and forward to the consummation of all things and
sees them both as the framework of the pattern. Less decorative

in purpose than Morris, Péguy sought to utilise every glimpse he got of grace at work on the warp of the world and to trace out its astonishing beauty.

'A kind of gardening in cloth' old Fuller called tapestry, and the figure fits Péguy's poetry well. It is a very french garden that emerges, formal, elaborate, rich, surprising by its ingenuity, satisfying in its elegance, replete with historical reminiscence. It suggests Chenonceaux or Chambord. It can also be somewhat wearisome to those who fail to approach it with stubborn attention and who miss the connection with the world of the spirit. The flat landscape of the Beauce unrolls:

> Where nothing hides the man standing before God's face,
> This plain where no disguise, whether of time or place,
> Can save the prey who from the heavenly hunter flies.

Whether it is gardening or pilgrimage, all has been turned into praying:

> Here is the firmament and all else is feigning,
> And, before the judgment, here is an agreement,
> And before Paradise, here is an achievement.

This is inescapable since the whole earthly terrain is Christ's inheritance and nearly two hundred quatrains will spell out the items of it:

> Il allait hériter de l'école stoïque.
> Il allait hériter de l'héritier romain. Il allait hériter du laurier héroique.
> Il allait hériter de tout l'effort humain. [1]

---

1. He was going to inherit the Stoic school.
   He was going to inherit the legacy of Rome.
   He was going to inherit the hero's laurel-wreath.
   He was going to inherit all human undertaking.

Péguy promised to put everything that mattered in and he kept
his word. The gardening too is part of the praying since nothing,
says God, is so fine in all my creation as the garden of souls that
Frenchmen have made:
    'Peuple jardinier, qui as fait pousser les plus belles fleurs de
sainteté.' [2] and so,
    'Français, dit Dieu, c'est vous qui avez inventés ces beaux jar-
dins des âmes.' [3]
    It is not surprising that the Son of God appears in this tapestried
world as the Good Gardener himself, his work a more splendid
Eden, but the poet does not fail to give frenchmen their due:

'C'est vous qui dessinerez mes jardins de Paradis.' [4]

    Such tapestry, we soon learn, could be both woven and unroll-
ed world without end. It could both sustain and express the act of
praying. It takes up a number of themes, introduced with a
phrase repeated scores or hundreds of times, and plays with their
interaction with human history as long as the poet wills. The
motifs of a vast panel repeat as often as the design of the whole
allows. The man who prays them receives them at each repetition
with re-inforced significance and learns to use them as departure
points for new movements of prayer. In the *tapisserie* of Eve this
reaches epic proportions and embraces the whole world and its
history. It is easy to see why Teilhard de Chardin 'almost grudg-
ed' Péguy the subject of Eve, since it expresses in lyric-liturgical
form the burgeoning and unfolding of the universe to which he
himself was to devote his life's work, and which he recognised to
be Christ-centred like his own, and uttered with a perfect harmony of concrete and abstract features. What the *tapisserie* was
not was the kind of poem that Cecil Day-Lewis had in mind in
his own poem *On not saying Everything:*

2. 'Cultivating folk, who have raised the loveliest flowers of holiness.'
3. 'Frenchmen, says God, it is you who have made these true gardens of the spirit.'
4. 'It is you who will lay out the gardens of my paradise.'

Unwritten poems loom as if
They'd cover the whole of earthly life.
But each one, growing, learns to trim its
Impulse and meaning to the limits
Roughed out by me, then modified
In its own truth's expanding light.
A poem, settling to its form
Finds there's no jailer, but a norm
Of conduct, and a fitting sphere
Which stops it wandering everywhere.

We are set in the midst of so many and great wonders! This is the burden of the *tapisseries,* and Péguy spares no effort, no jot of his readers' attention to see them for what they are, in their majesty or their poverty, as flesh of our flesh. No poet could have emphasised the dignity and the mystery of the flesh more deliberately;

Il depend de nous chrétiennes
Que l'éternel ne manque point de temporel,
(Singulier renversement)
Que le spirituel ne manque point du charnel . . .
Que l'esprit ne manque point de chair
Que l'âme pour ainsi dire ne manque point de corps. [1]

yet none could have sung the creative-inventive work of the spirit with greater joy. He was not unmindful of the tensions of flesh and spirit, not insensible to the ravages of human sin, but he was even more possessed of faith in the redemptive work of Christ. It was the narrowness of so much that passed for christian vision that shocked him; it was the recognition of the wealth that

1. 'It rests with us christians
   That the eternal should not lack the temporal
   (Strange reversal)
   That the spirit should not be deprived of the carnal,
   That the spirit should not lack its flesh
   That the soul, so to say, should not be without its body.'

awaited discovery that caused him to exult. He was quite unafraid of the multiplicity and complexity of the created order. If
the inquiring spirit in man discovered a myriad hitherto unknown manifestations of 'la chair', all the more reason for rejoicing over them. If in the bleak light of the aftermath of the
Enlightenment the explorers themselves could see little more
than the flesh, a tragic and fearful failing of vision, it was due to a
temporary failure of the clerks. They were so often afraid where
no fear was!

So when Péguy came to honour Ste. Geneviève there was a
good deal to say about *les armes de Satan,* but much more about *les
armes de Jésus,* much to be said about the squalor and wealth,
about the horrors and achievements, not forgetting such details as
the metre and the gramme, not even citizens like Renan and
Taine! Paris was infinitely rich. There are times when the tone
suggests Whitman who in a more raucous fashion had set out to
sing the american continent as it was being 'discovered' by his
ebullient generation. It is easy to make fun of its catalogue-verse,
to object to its hectoring voice, but the poet's task, as Péguy saw
it, was to face, absorb, contain and rejoice in this rush of things,
this *jaillissement* of a new age, to give it the order it needed, to
subdue it to the spirit. It was a task for a poet whose imagination
would wrestle with such exuberance of the flesh in Christ's name.
Péguy was not to be daunted by it.

The choice of the word *mystère* to characterise his longer
poems, like the use of *mystique* in political matters, sprang from
his sense of engaging himself and his work with the ultimate
mystery of God. It still needs saying perhaps that mystery here
means not a puzzle or problem to be solved but a truth which
outstretches yet commands the attention of the human mind,
defies discovery while it courts it, evokes veneration while it
offers itself to be known by the least of its creatures. Mystery
breaks into the mental world of mankind unannounced, a
hairsbreadth dividing its blinding and illuminating power. It embraces God and man. In moments of confrontation men see and
hear-for the senses seem fused into one-some glimpse or utterance
of a reality curtained off from ordinary life. To attempt to speak

of what they have seen or heard they are forced to use such symbols devised in the deepest levels of their own being as lend themselves to the task. Contradictions persist. Too holy to be spoken of, a mystery compels expression; too vast to be contained in words it kneads a language to its purpose. The ladder itself is one of many such symbols men have used to utter the changed perception that has overtaken a man. In religions mystery has extended its grasp to rites and objects that can express the illumination given anew to birth and rebirth, to hunger and satisfaction, to love and death.

Religious symbols are needed to give meaning to the continuing presence of mystery in man's life. The moments of mystical vision without the symbols would soon

> fall
> Like a bright exhalation in the evening
> And no man see me more.

The symbol, however inadequately, conveys the numinous experience, the sense of awe, of being confronted by an unbidden unbiddable event, as Jacob was at the ford of Jabbok. It acknowledges something to be adored, it knows exaltation in being caught up in such an experience at all. The line between the conception that a man had of himself and the world beyond has shifted, the ground on which he stands is changed, he is 'a man beside himself' yet never more truly himself than now. He is abased and lifted up, annihilated and re-created by what has taken place. The numinous may suggest being present to or in the presence of a person or power from whom all things proceed. It has been compared to looking into a revealing mirror, such a mirror as Michael Ayrton spoke of into which God gazed as the spirit hovered over the face of the waters at creation's dawn.

Mystery is central to Péguy's work, not as a matter of brief moments of mystical vision but as a continuing act of brooding over man's life thus engaged with God. He is seeing as he is seen. He is living embraced by mystery itself. He turns to it as a lover. In a generation of men who were discarding, and priding themselves upon so discarding the mystery of the christian faith, Péguy sought it the more intensely. His *mystères* are the record of his attachment to it ever in process of renewal. His poetry and his prayer are two aspects of one unwearied seeking, and if we at times grow tired of some phrase he repeats many hundred times, it is well that we should think of it as the kind of importunate knocking that Christ promised would lead to opening of doors.

Péguy's symbols have their own *jaillissement* out of the homeliest stock of human experience, out of his childhood's storehouse of such things as wiping his boots on coming in or watching a carpenter choosing the piece of wood he needs or carefully folding his clothes. The resonance of such things stays with him all his life, whereas most of us grow deaf. Beneath them all was the familiar mortice and tenon joint, the temporal and eternal fitted together, which must be looked to. 'Do away with that link,' he said, 'and there is nothing left'. It has been restated in many ways by others. For Péguy it meant that all history was to be seen from that conjunction, all work and politics and art were dependent for their truth upon it. Christ was that intersecting point of heaven and earth, of time and eternity.

> Miracle des miracles, mon enfant, mystère des mystères.
> Parce que Jésus-Christ est devenu notre frère charnel . . .
> C'est à nous, infirmes, qu'il a été donné,
> C'est de nous qu'il depend, infirmes et charnels,
> De faire vivre et de nourrir et de garder vivantes dans le temps
> Ces paroles prononcees vivantes dans le temps.
> Mystère des mystères, ce privilège nous a été donné. [1]

---

1. 'Wonder of wonders, my child, mystery of mysteries,
   That Jesus Christ is become our brother in the flesh.
   That to us, weak creatures, He has been given thus,
   That on us, sensual and frail, He should depend,
   For bearing, nourishing, tending in time
   Words spoken, living and alive in time.
   Mystery of mysteries, this honour has been ours.'

It was no novelty thought up by the poet but the faith of the Christian Church. What was new was the determined embodiment of it in Péguy's life and work. At a time when the reach of that faith was shrinking fast, he proclaimed the reverse. He would show it embracing all, and he meant all. *Le Mystère de la Deuxième Vertu* repeats over and over again that it is the Father's will that none of these least should perish. God waits and trembles and hopes that it will be so. This lost sheep, this dying soul, has moved the heart of God like this,

> Elle a fait trembler le coeur de Dieu
> Du tremblement même de l'espérance.
> Elle a introduit au coeur même de Dieu la théologale
> Espérance. [2]

None of it can be taken for granted. All the strain and fear that waits upon a choice to be made, all the delight that surrounds a decision made, comes into each daily renewal of man's relation to God. Péguy's vision of France and frenchmen, his battles with politicians and clerks, his passion for Joan and the saints, were all part of such a *mystère*. He wrote his poems to pray out his involvement in it.

In a secondary sense the mysteries which in the medieval world grew out of the liturgy of the Church and from which the drama of Western Europe may be said to have grown, have their bearing on Péguy's work. They had drawn out in dramatic form the events of God's action in time in the life, death and resurrection of Jesus Christ. They were thrust aside and largely forgotten as Renaissance drama came to focus attention upon men and women caught up in the narrower world of their own choices. The old mysteries played out the play before God and man, the new drama played to a human audience only. Péguy set God once again in the audience, in the darkness beyond the footlights; he set Him also among the players, in the scenes to be played and the

2. 'This soul has moved the very heart of God
   Making it tremble with hope indeed.
   It carried into God's heart the godly hope.'

words to be said. It was after all His play. Not unexpectedly then it is God the Father who speaks throughout the greater part of Péguy's mysteries but His voice is that of a man's father, of one who watches and enters into all parts in the play yet will have men play it out for themselves. Monologue it must be but filled with such exclamations of wonder and joy and pain that all voices are speaking through Him. God is astonished to see how men play their parts, astonished to see what His grace can do with them.

With such an expression of divine delight in the virtue hope. Péguy began the *Mysteries of the Holy Innocents* and the *Second Virtue*. *Cette petite espérance* appears in both poems as a little girl, the youngest sister, who causes the old father to cry out with astonishment and joy. 'I am not easily astonished', says God, 'I am old and have seen much', but He continues to watch this child who darts about, taking her part in processions with her grown-up sisters faith and love, skipping with pleasure, running twenty times further than she need, herself the great promise of life, the sign and seal of the triumph of God's grace.

It is the note on which two such diverse creatures as Ernst Bloch and Charles Péguy come together, the one to which they both constantly return. The past weighs heavily upon mankind, the present is opaque and doubtful, but man is not bound by these; he is the hoper, the one ready to make the leap, the one whose grasp of the moment of wonder frees him to go forward.

'Child, yesterday's journey is done, think about tomorrow's.' There is no limit to the imagery with which hope can be celebrated. The crown of thorns turns into *une couronne de verdure, une couronne éternelle.* The bud of promise breaks through the hard wrinkled bark of an old tree. 'It is my little hope who sleeps well, who greets mankind with a good-day, who says her prayers with new attention.' Without hope the Night would fall at last covering up both the primal murder and the gibbets of Calvary. But hope changes all and 'makes a new morning spring from an old yesterday.'

Fundamental to Péguy's poetry is the goodness of the creation and God's pleasure in it. Men's sins have ravaged it and much

brutal insensibility has thrust from sight the wealth of its diversity. Growing unresponsive to it men grow bored with themselves
and each other. *Ennui* eats out the heart of human enterprise as
men fail to grow in a sense of wonder. Péguy's poetry is by contrast a sustained celebration charged with radical amazement at
the originality of God. He is always seeing things 'as clean and
new as on the starting day'; always handling them with an in-
quiry — what does this mean? what does that do? what part has
this played in life? what does this yield to others? Eternity is
plainly too short to finish the enumeration but that is at least how
it is best spent.

It is to be noted further that this most personal poetry has at all
times the objectivity that marks the great early christian hymns.
The fundamental 'isness' of things is supreme for while Péguy
had the romantic hunger for the radiance attached to things that
dispelled for ever any sense that 'That's all there is to know', he
did not depend upon feelings or moods about them. He is the
poet as described by the words of Keats: 'the most unpoetical of
anything in existence, because he has no identity; he is continually in for, and filling, some other body'. 'As my imagination
strengthens' went on Keats in another letter, 'I do not live in this
world alone, but in a thousand worlds. No sooner am I alone,
than shapes of epic greatness are stationed around me and serve
my spirit the office which is equivalent to a King's Bodyguard;
then "Tragedy with scepter'd pall comes sweeping by"; according to my state of mind I am with Achilles shouting in the
trenches, or with Theocritus in the vales of Sicily.'

That too was Péguy's life, filled on the one hand with all that
omniverous reading gave him, on the other with his own notic-
ing of grain trickling beneath the millstones, a sleeping child's
eyelashes resting upon its cheeks, a woman setting down a lamp
upon the supper table. It was the immensity of God's providence
that kept him utterly astonished. What he set out to do was to
help men to recover a heritage that through ignorance and
wilfulness, through pride and folly, had been so roughly
squandered. The poet's task was what Vincent van Gogh had
once said of his own work — 'to put the radiance to human beings

that was expressed by the old haloes', but not to human beings only. It meant taking God at His word that 'All that I have is thine' and so renewing a world of wonder.

It is such vision as this that underlies Péguy's lines upon childhood and innocence in *Le Mystère des Saints Innocents*. Its base is simple pleasure. 'They please me, God says, and that is enough.' It then goes down to the depths for these children were murdered, and their like have been tortured and maimed all down the ages. 'They resemble my Son.' It climbs to the heights because they are lovely as the red flowers of the apple, because they have no lines at the corners of their mouths, because they are the blossom of the hawthorn that flowers in Holy Week. "There they resemble the Lamb in his eternal Glory." Péguy had no illusions about the wear and tear of the world:

> Happy is he who remains like a child
> And who like a child keeps
> His first innocence

but he knew what losses as well as gains had to be endured. He put it starkly enough by saying that the adult could not invent a child's saying, could not even remember it though desperately wanting to do so. 'It has vanished from your memory. It is too pure a water and has slipped away from your muddy memory.' Yet, he insisted, that saying struck into the adult world like a voice from another creation, from a world where you once were, and as it was heard, you listened to your former soul. Be the fruit what it may, these are the flowers without which there will be no fruit at all. 'Before the soul is exalted, it is humbled.' Péguy could see no truer humbling in hope than the lives of the children themselves. 'Such is my paradise, says God, it could not be simpler. Nothing is less elaborate than my paradise . . . children playing in its streets and on the altar steps.'

We can perhaps see Péguy better if we compare him with one who has gained far greater fame, who did his military service in Orléans a year or two before Péguy, and who set himself the task of seeking within the former self or selves that which each of us has been. Writing of Proust, Maurois described this voyage of discovery within ourselves, pointing out that it is not made by the deliberate effort of memory·set methodically to climb up and down the infinite staircase of time, but by the use of some evocative power of a sensation which restores to consciousness a vanished life. Something which seemed to have been for ever lost might be recalled by tapping the associations of sight, smell and sound and touch. Some few rare spirits might retain capacity to utilise the long-buried past in this way. Péguy's approach was more sure-footed and robust. It was not by such acts of recall however made that he set out to gain the freshness of the early world. The line of Victor Hugo's that he is said to have loved:

> 'Mes soeurs, l'onde est plus fraîche aux premiers feux du
> jour.' [1]

pointed not backward but forward to a life that had yet to be laid hold of. Péguy would have understood fully Nietzsche's contention that maturity lay in recovering the seriousness that one had known as a child; he put it into practice by learning to be himself.

> But truly happy is the man who is a child, who remains a
> child,
> Strictly, precisely, the child that he himself was,
> Because truly it has been granted to everyman to be.

The subject of Péguy's poetry, line by line, is what God does. Sometimes the speaking voice shifts to human beings like Joan or Madame Gervaise but the poetry is what God hears; if Péguy appears to be speaking himself it is what God knows, if the fields of France are being described they are what God sees. All Péguy's poetry is a God-centred act of reflection and celebration. It is therefore exposed to enormous risks. It will have the most glaring faults. Was it just presumptuous folly to attempt to write

1. 'Sisters, the sea is freshest at the break of day.'

in that way? I believe that we need to try to follow Peguy's
life-long choice as fully as we can. Remember that he chose to do
it that way because he believed that what mattered most at the
time he wrote was getting that conjunction of God and man
firmly renewed and both known and seen to be the great axis or
centre of the turning world. He took poetry to be the serious
creative thing that Coleridge had claimed it to be, and that meant
seeking to use it to declare the creative purpose at work here and
now in our midst. Péguy did not falter. His faults are those of
clumsiness but his intention was maintained throughout. He
would make known that ever particle of dust, every act in time,
every word that was conceived and uttered had its bearing upon
God. What was needed was the poet's work to recall men to that
truth, to help them see it as the truth, to bind them closer to the
recognition of it.

No word more truly expresses what he set out to do, and what
we in reading Péguy need to keep in mind, than the liturgical
word *anamnesis*. Of its character in relation to poetry David Jones
has since Péguy's time written fully in his *Epoch and Artist*.
No-one, I think, has more plainly said what this God-centred
poetry struggles to do. Speaking of his own poem *Anathemata* he
wrote: 'What I have written has no plan, or at least is not planned. If it has a shape it is chiefly that it returns to its beginnings'.
Anamnesis means not the recalling of things past by an act of
memory but the re-presentation of things done and said that they
may be here and now operative in our midst. It is the heart of the
poetic and sacramental understanding of life, the bedrock of
christian faith. Péguy did not permit himself to be shifted from
that task. Jones spoke of his work as 'accomplishing an actual
journey, and changing the figure, pointed to the Jacob's ladder
that reaches from all perishable things, including those over
which the minister is directed to say "bless, ascribe to, sanctify,
make reasonable and acceptable", to that point of intersection as
it has been called where these things are made as clean and new as
on the starting day.'

At the centre, at the heart, everything is realised,

everything is consummated by my Son.
And it is retold for me.
And there is a recall, an echo, a reminder and as it were a
    return.

It was in the strength of that vision that Péguy lived and worked. His intention was always that by learning to pray he and his
fellow-men might come to that centre too.

8. 'Approfondissement'

'How with this rage shall beauty hold a plea,
Whose action is no stronger than a flower.'
                                    William Shakespeare, *Sonnet LXV*.

'Birth is a desperate business, and rebirth even more so.'
                                    John Russell, *Francis Bacon*.

Péguy did not live long into the 20th century. He went down
early into one of those mass graves which have become expressive monuments of our time. He would not have wished it
otherwise:

> Happy are those who die, for they are enfolded
> Into the primitive clay.

What that clay meant to him we have seen in part already. His
love for the soil of France was of that character that he could not
have embraced it in life as perfectly as he did in death. The
sacramental vision of the world which he cherished was so complete that living and dying in it were equally acts of participation
in its response to God. He had written of 'a just war' as a condition of happiness for those thus called upon to die, but it was war
stripped of qualifications that broke out and swept him and many
millions to their death. His work was done.

> Enter my night as into my house. For there I have
>   reserved
> The right to be master.

and it could be said without doubt that Péguy had been pressing
forward to that entrance as into a home where he was expected.
His prayer sustained him as he made the journey.

I have said earlier that the word *jaillissement* expressed so much
of what Péguy rejoiced to believe of the nature of life, of God's
quickening presence in it, of God's inexhaustible vitality there. It
was his own picture of the well of water springing up to eternal
life. He so lived in expectation of it that it lent to all his work its
sharp questioning, hopeful, even reckless character. This *jaillissement* had its counterpart in reverse, in *approfondissement* which
never ceases to try to penetrate more deeply into the truth in
God. With these two words our Péguy has written his own brief
version of that upward and downward journey which St. John of
the Cross had described in his reflections upon the secret ladder.
The two words taken together must shape all our understanding
of his life in prayer.

'I incline to believe', wrote Caroline Spurgeon, in her book on
Shakespeare's imagery, 'that analogy-likeness between dissimilar
things – which is the fact underlying the possibility and reality of
metaphor – holds within itself the very secret of the universe.'
She was describing as briefly as possible the nature of the work of
a poet who, as Coleridge had said 'brought the whole soul into
activity' by the power of imagination, a work not by any means
limited to the furnishing of images but one in which the imagery
did lay bare 'the furniture of his mind, the channels of his
thought, the objects and incidents he observes and remembers,
and perhaps most significant of all, those which he does not
observe or remember.'

The bearing of such use of imagery upon praying is profound.
Prayer, with its silences and its words, is the supreme form of
communication, ever stretching its resources and expending its
energy to bring those involved in it more wholly into communion with each other. Addressed to God, it strives to give ever
more and more adequate expression to its grasp of reality, to strip
off whatever is jargon or cant or cliché, to come clean and make
all things new. It acknowledges its own insufficiencies but persists
in its intentions. *Toujours l'audace.* 'I will speak yet once more.' Its

importunity presses upon language itself no less than upon time. What is begotten of its consummations is new life for the spirit embodied again and again in new metaphors which are 'lived through', sounded out, and often exhausted by generations of common use. Such imagery was richly present in Péguy's poetry.

Approfondissement is such a key image. It sums up as far as one word can do, as far as a life can be so summed up, what Péguy meant by a life of prayer. It sums up further what he understood of his whole life's work as a poet. *Approfondissement* embraces it all. He did not change the direction of his life, he simply deepened it. He did not develop new ideas or embrace a new philosophical outlook, but dug deeper into the faith that he confessed. He took very literally and seriously what is implied in the Old Testament prophets' perception of God's presence in the human heart. 'It was', he wrote 'by a continual deepening of the heart along the same path, and not as the result of an "evolution", in no sense by retracing our steps, that we found the christian path. We did not find it by turning back. We found it at the end.' What that meant could only be known to Péguy as the years of effort yielded their burden of vision, and it is for this reason that the poem *Eve* appears as the great representative and expressive work of his life. He knew it indeed to be such. It is the sustained deep-digging that will not be stayed. It presses beyond the pagans and saints, beyond the Lord's mother herself, to find her whom Jesus addresses, the mother buried outside the primal garden.

> Et moi je vous salue ô la première femme
> Et la plus malheureuse et la plus décevante
> Et la plus immobile et la plus émouvante,
> Aïeule aux longs cheveux, mère de Notre Dame.[1]

---

1. 'And I myself hail you, O earliest woman,
   Most hapless and most deceptive,
   Most unshaken, most moving,
   Ancestress with wild long hair, mother of Our Lady.'

If we ask what it is that Péguy found by thus pursuing the processes of *approfondissement* he himself will tell us. He found the communion of which we have spoken. 'Jesus belongs to the same world as the last of sinners; and the last of sinners belongs to the same world as Jesus, *c'est une communion.*' There, in his poem the mother of the race and Jesus are together. She, so pitiably deceived, so cruelly wounded, is His mother. He has come into her world and made it all His own, redeeming it and her. *Eve* could not but be a very long poem. It is man's history, *le long ressouvenir de son vagabondage,*[1] and the poet was quite unwilling to permit a fragment of it to be discarded or thrown away. He is a man looking at the home in which he has lived and brought up his own family. There is not a thing in it however worn and soiled and broken which has not played its part in their lives together, which is not expressive of their loves and hates, their fears and hopes, which is not sacramental for that reason. *C'est une communion.* Tomorrow the sale may disperse them all, the children may be gone, the bull-dozer obliterate the house, but now, in this moment when eternity grips it with eternal Love, there is time to see it bathed in a radiance that is His. There is time, if we so will, for our prayers to handle our own brief bit of this vagabondage in such a fashion that it too may disclose the eternal glory. As Hardy wrote,

> Yet an iris at that season
>   Amid the accustomed slight
> From denseness, dull unreason,
>   Ringed me with living light.

None is so poor as to lack that opportunity.

What *approfondissement* meant on an even wider scale Péguy also made clear. *Eve* is not simply a poetical version of the phenomenon of man but a descent into the spiritual depths of human experience, below those many distinctions and divisions which men have devised for the practical purposes of living,

---

1. 'The long remembrance of his vagrancy.'

below those serviceable constructions of history, theology, liturgy, poetics, which like all servants tend to become masters, to find the pure potentiality of things, diversity in unity as yet unhardened, unity in diversity exuberant in its wealth. The distinctions are observed, the divisions are erased. 'One of the immediate results' wrote Péguy, 'is the disappearance of any arbitrary separation of abstract and concrete. The abstract is immediately nourished by the concrete, and the concrete illuminated by the abstract.' Péguy's understanding of the catholic faith was thus rooted in experience of that deep interchange. It sounded the depths of both cultural triumph and barbarous waste. It was the reconciliation of order and freedom. 'All the resources of nature and grace are gathered together and harvested at the feet of God.'

'Tout le jaillissement dans le germe, tout l'ordre dans l'epi.' *Approfondissement* was the reaping process.

I have emphasised throughout this book that while Péguy loved those quick flashes of insight, those recognitions of what God was doing which were to him especially french, he was in his own work cautious, deliberate and slow, quite unwilling to permit himself or anyone else to suppose that praying so conceived could ever be anything else but a laborious scouring out of the channels of grace. To our age of speed and instant functioning, Péguy is an impenitent footslogger. He speaks most characteristically when he talks of beginning again. 'One is eternally beginning again. Only after the Last Judgement will beginning again come to an end. Prayer is always a beginning over again.' To a world excited by its own programmes of planned change and progress it sounds absurd and worse. Yet each of us wants it to be true of ourselves, to be found to be the truth of our life.

Péguy was always ready to face the lowest stair, not as a man defeated but as one who exults in having kept his course. He holds unshakeably to his conviction that God Himself is always beginning again with His people and will never cease to do so. 'Where is it written,' he cries, 'that God will abandon man in sin?' Theology may tell us that God is in need of nothing, but the

wisdom of the heart delves deeper. A man needs his sons. God
needs his children. 'Dieu a besoin de nous, Dieu a besoin de sa
créature', and God's grace will not be thwarted. It will accomplish what it sets out to do 'cette renaissante, cette
perpétuellement renaissante, cette éternellement renaissante
nouveauté.'

We miss the significance of it if we suppose that we can
become onlookers only at such a mystery. Prayer is the necessary
recommitment of ourselves to what is being done by Christ in
His world, to the pain and suffering it entails no less than to the
joy. Exultation in the eyes and mouths of those freed from bonds,
certainly, but who knows with what pain as the quickened life
courses through channels once closed and dead? What bewilder-
ment goes with the first steps of limbs so lately paralysed? There
is a magnificent picture in the *Mystery of the Holy Innocents* of the
great fleets of praying advancing upon God behind the strong
prow of 'Our Father which art in Heaven':

> As cranes fly in a triangle upwards,
> And in this way go where they will,
> Cleaving the air and driving back the power of the wind
> itself.

so prayer bears down upon God. 'From the throne of my eternal
greatness I see rising towards me the fleet which assails me.' But
then Péguy can be quite explicit about his own agony in the
matter. 'Would you believe', he wrote to an intimate friend,
'that for eighteen months I could not say Our Father? Thy will
be done was quite impossible to say. Can you understand it? I
could not accept His will. It is terrifying. Prayer isn't a matter of
trickling off a few prayers. You have really to mean what you
say. I could not really mean "Thy will be done". It was an impossibility. It was still more impossible to say "Forgive me my
trespasses as I forgive".'

1. 'God needs us, God needs his creatures.'
2. 'this reborn, this endlessly reborn, this eternally reborn new creation.'

Péguy is to be trusted because he did not disguise from himself
and his friends the fact that the most devoted of lives could come
to such an impasse. He encountered the problem early and expressed it in the anguish of Joan. Only by a sustained act of *approfondissement* could christian faith continue to embrace the
world and await the renewal of re-creation. At each turning of
the stair he knew himself to be exposed to new versions of the
problem. In each encounter 'a terrible beauty' was disclosed.
They came to him as a young man becoming aware of the
age-long suffering of the poor and weak; they came to the
mature man as daily battles to maintain integrity in a milieu
where *politique* warred upon *mystique*. They came to him as the
end approached, in the haunting lines of Eve,

> 'Heureux ceux qui sont morts pour quatre coins de
> terre.'[1]

Lines in which the word *mort* reverberates like the sound of the
great bell Emmanuel in the tower of Notre Dame. It was part of
the inheritance;

> He was going to inherit all that can be bequeathed
> And of the man who has nothing, Jesus is the sole heir.
> He was going to begin the great coming,
> The coming of God to the heart of each man.

Approfondissement is anything but leaden-footed. It seeks and
knows a vivacious freedom. 'Man is a strange creature, says God,
for in him operates that liberty which is the mystery of mysteries
– my greatest invention – but I know how to take him.' This is
not quite the tone or idiom of the *Hound of Heaven,* though Péguy
was ready to slip in a remark about hunting the fox to make the
taking more gamesome. God elsewhere speaks again in similar
fashion. 'Do you think that I enjoy setting traps for you, as if I
were the King of the Savages? The only cunning I practice is the

---

1. 'Happy are those who die for four quarters of the earth.'

cunning of my grace, which often plays the sinner for his salvation.'

In both the *Mystères* the imagery of fatherhood is teased out into an endless variety of playful comments. God is the father who delights in playing with his children, who laughs with them as they lie laughing in his arms, who smiles at the ideas that rattle in their heads like seeds in a pumpkin given to them to play with. His pleasure grows the more as he watches his children learning to play their own game, to take risks, to exercise skill, to make decisions, to play out the play to the end. 'I have often played with man, says God, but what a game! It is a game that makes me tremble yet. I have often played with man, but, by God, it was in order to save him. I often play against man, says God, but it is he who wants to lose, the fool, and it is I who want him to win.'

It is not altogether the image of God acceptable in Geneva or serious-minded Boston, but we must start with this playfulness if we are to get anywhere near the way Péguy prayed. This is no fanciful way of writing, no failure to observe the advice of Peter Porter's cat − 'don't make your poem seem too twee' − but imagination playing with the realities of human life in a way that tests the validity of imagination itself.

Two generations ago it is doubtful if the idea of prayer and the spiritual life seen in terms of playing a game or playing a fish − despite the call to be fishers of men − would have gained much favour. It would have seemed to many too flippant a way to approach things sacred and sublime. Play was a matter for the immature, recreation an escape from duties, theatrical playing still suspect. Not many would have been ready to see scientific work in that light either or foreseen the day when Jacob Bronowski would conclude his survey of the *Ascent of Man* with an account of John von Neumann's theory of games. Even fewer would have welcomed the jester, as the Marxist philosopher Kolakowski does, as one needed to shake men's stabilised systems. They had scarcely heard or perhaps forgotten Pascal's words advising them to stop looking for certainty and stability and to prepare themselves to accept the gamble of faith.

'You wish to attain faith, but do not know the way,' Pascal had written, 'you would like to cure yourself of unbelief, and you ask the remedy for it. Learn of those who have been bound like you, and who now stake all their possessions'. With card-players in mind he went on to insist 'you must wager, you must make the bet of faith', and criticised no less a person than St. Augustine for failing to admit that man was under compulsion to accept the odds against him. Daily life presented a variety of such wagers but none more important than the choice between God and nothing. 'Who chooseth me, must give and hazard all he hath.' As often as that *me* appeared to be the figure on the cross, it was understandable that many chose fairer shapes. Péguy who pondered deeply on Pascal's *Pensées* must often have paused at this: 'If this discourse pleases you and seems impressive, know that it is made by a man who has knelt, both before and after it, in prayer to that Being, infinite and without parts, before whom he lays all he has, for you also to lay before Him all you have for your own good and His glory that so strength may be given to lowliness'.

'Who now stake all.' Péguy took that bet of christian faith as Pascal meant it to be taken: now, this day and every day. As often as what seemed a familiar road twisted to disclose new features, to make new demands, the bet had to be made again, with a cry of terror or a gasp of delight. 'For your whole apparatus' he wrote in the first Clio *Cahier,* 'is built and founded on there being a risk, a total risk: man must make his choice in absolute freedom. There must therefore, in the last analysis, be a risk. One always comes back to the bet . . . The risk must be preserved, integrally. That, my child, is christianity. C'est une gageure.'

We should miss the whole point of this if we failed to perceive the intensity with which it was made. Péguy's praying took on the bet of christian faith with a seriousness that makes human life threaten to explode at any moment with the revelation of God. 'I explode, says God, in plants, in animals, in the beasts of the forest, and in man, my creation.' Prayer as Péguy then understood it was a matter of learning to live in such an explosive world, of living expectantly. Where so much turns on the bet of faith to be made today, into what depths must a man descend to wrest from himself such a choice?

Péguy has rightly been called, with the Beatitudes in mind, a desperately hungry man. He was often a very tired and angry one, breaking with friends and lashing out at opponents with uncompromising fury. What he experienced was the two-fold act of submission, 'I can no other' and 'I can no more', repeated day after day, not in any spectacular fashion but all the more self-committing for being a hidden process. 'The christian, christianity, christendom, is not a public operation, a superficial, historical operation; it is not a public event. It is a secret event, a profound, inward operation, and often, the more profound it is the less it modifies external aspects and appearances.'

So his praying became the expectant act of one who scans the horizon in hope, the horizon which lies deep in the human soul. 'In depth' has become a commonplace phrase of our time. Men have learned to converse about the various strata of being, peered into the abyss, reported the unconscious, made news of the underworld itself. The experts in the field have bored deep into the sources of man's nature; the fierce and often violent unformed stuff of potential spiritual life that has shot up flaming in our midst. The seismic tremors of interior struggles have been charted, the age-old symbols of unconscious impulse catalogued and noted. A famous photograph taken at the Congress of Psychoanalysis at Weimar in 1911 which shows Freud, Stekel and Jung to the fore, reminds us how recently such a knowledge has been gained.

Péguy did not despise knowledge though he made constant attacks on pretentious professions of it. His own concern was with a knowledge in depth of a quite different kind, with a *milieu divin* in which a personal relationship had to be honoured throughout. It was his business to be both wholly sensitive to the world and its pressures on human life and resistant to its control. He must translate those pressures into spiritual terms in the depths of his own life, discern between good and evil in them, and carry on the conflict as the occasion demanded. Pascal was in his mind throughout, the Pascal who had written, 'Jesus will be in agony even to the end of the world. We must not sleep during that time.' Péguy would not have expressed it in that way – sleep had its place among God's greatest gifts – but he knew what Pascal wanted. Praying was being awake when the time of demand came along. You dug down to discover the place of encounter. Men were always being tempted to settle for something less disturbing, for something that promised protection rather than a fresh exposure to the pressures of God in His world. 'Place yourself in the presence of God', St. François de Sales had written as his primary counsel to those setting out to pray, and Péguy would have said as much but warned men that it was no easy option.

Approfondissement was then the summing up in a single word of all that Péguy as poet and man of prayer was concerned to practice. It may be used to describe what I believe to be the most important task now confronting the christian church – as a representative of all mankind – the task of bringing to birth and nourishing a spirituality strong, generous and inspiring enough to help men and women, the world over, to grow up as truly human beings in the immensely complicated world that lies ahead. That spirituality must provide a disciplined way of living in which each person is acknowledged to be needed and contributory to the lives of others, in which the freedom and growth to the fullest possible stature of each is made the concern of all, in which the inner and outer life is nurtured by responsible use of all the resources that mankind has at its disposal; a spirituality which takes its Trinitarian imagery more seriously than ever before, relating the creativity, the humanising and the unification of mankind in one growing experience of mutual love. The world may well be entering a yet darker dark age than any known before. The demands laid on the spirituality needed during such time will be correspondingly greater. The constructive task in terms of this ladder for man's spiritual journey upwards and downwards is determined by it.

The marks of such spirituality were discerned by Péguy. The first is that of amplitude; not the gross multiplication of things but the containment and bearing of the widest diversity of human life within human love. Péguy's imagery was distinctly feminine. 'A woman who will also be a saint' summed up his hope for the future. In the meanwhile he gazed as attentively as he could, going back as far as Eve, at the revelations of femininity to be noted and taken to heart. 'In a generous womb once dwelling' focussed the basic conviction upon which all hopes must rest. The Word did, does and will become flesh and dwell among men. Mankind needed to learn all over again the character of expectation which it once symbolised in Christ's mother. Men had done much by imposing an ordered structure upon life; it was the necessary foundation for all foundations whatever, and all these Péguy honoured.

But there was also another thing needed if the structures were not to become either prisons or follies. The wisdom of the body, the wisdom of the heart, had also to be listened to. The brooding over the yet unformed had to be repeated if the miracle of creativity were to continue in time. 'Creativity is always linked with the happy moment when all conscious control can be forgotten.' 'According to thy word' spelled out the essential truth. The meaning of the word, 'present yet not present', required an amplitude of spirit, humbled to its task, joyful in its expectation of mutuality and diversity, ungrudgingly welcoming of what must be infinitely costly. Amplitude waited upon intimations of transcendence, and made room for them.

The second feature must be that of imagination. The needed spirituality must be freed on the one hand from dead externalised imagery which can only enslave men's minds and make them fearful and cruel in turn, and sensitised to a new and deeper awareness of all that art and poetry can make known to man of his spiritual stature and his engagement with God. The imagination of the poet is needed to hold together 'the mighty opposites' that men must face in living, for where it is lacking men project their fears of the uncontrollable world, within and without themselves, upon those dwelling with them. 'The displaced person today is a pathetic image of the illness that has befallen our body social, namely its inability to tolerate diversity without undue anxiety.' It was part of Péguy's task to help men to see that the problems of First, Second and Third Worlds confronting each other were not simply conflicts of economic or political interests, though these were operative in them, but conflicts between divergent images of man himself, as old as Oedipus and Abraham, as new as Dostoyevsky's Man from the Underworld or Kafka's K. *Approfondissement* meant nothing less than a new resolution of ancient issues appearing in as yet unrecognised guise.

Yet while needing the help of artists and poets to carry men boldly to new rungs of the ladder, men must learn also to act imaginatively with each other in the families and groupings into which they came or were drawn. An imaginative process was needed, a cultivation of the garden of souls, not dependent upon one leader or an élite or an ecclesiastical ministry, but 'compacted by that which every part supplied'. A cultural solidarity continually refreshed by imaginative effort of all those who participated in it would be the true basis for new ventures of faith.

Péguy would have understood completely what Troeltsch meant when, having surveyed the social teaching of the christian churches in the past, he looked forward to what lay ahead. 'If the present social situation is to be mastered by christian principles thoughts will be necessary which have not been thought and which will correspond to this new situation as the older forms corresponded to the older situations. These thoughts will have to be drawn from the interior spontaneity of the christian idea.' A world that threatened to become a Waste Land in which there was 'not even silence in the mountains' could be redeemed only by recourse to that interior.

> Mystère des mystères, portant sur les mystères mêmes,
> Il a mis en nos mains, en nos faible mains, son espérance
> éternelle![1]

It depended upon such hands to lead others there.

[1] 'Mystery of mysteries, conveying mystery itself,
    He has put into our hands, our weak hands, mystery itself.'

The third feature was that of fidelity. The word rings through all that Péguy wrote, and he used it as the touchstone of every decision he made in politics or family affairs or intellectual work. He deprecated turning it into something heroic and preferred to speak of it in terms of a craftsman choosing a piece of wood for the job to be done. It was matter of fact and infinitely costly. Any english parish priest who has worked in a working-class parish will have heard it said of someone's facing of that kind of decision, 'He had it to do'. It is not resignation or apathy but a considered sense of responsibility, of fidelity to the calling of being human. As Pierre Charles wrote in his meditation upon what is sung upon the steps: 'If we do not go up to the top, it was useless to have begun the ascent, each step involves the one to follow it a little more imperiously'. Péguy was once described as a man who sang at the back of his throat like a peasant; he sang on all the steps of this upward-downward ladder, knowing that there was neither a turning-back nor a surrender of purpose in *approfondissement*. He pictured the farmer ploughing in the failed harvest and setting out to do the job all over again. 'I have treasures of grace' he said, and went on his way.

> Nothing is so fine as fidelity which has withstood all tests.
> Nothing is so fine as courage displayed in isolation.

The fourth feature is that of freedom; a freedom of spirit that made a man likest to God in whose image he had been formed. It made him also concerned with liberation of all who were oppressed or enslaved. What Péguy understood in terms of *approfondissement* here was a continual searching out of all those things which denied or curtailed the freedom of men and women. It meant unwearied observation to catch sight of those 'whom Satan hath bound', to hear the pleas of those who had no voice to make themselves heard. If men failed to hear the prayers of men for such liberation, how could they be free as a matter of grace?

The fifth feature confronts us with the costliness of it all. *Ap-*

profondissement makes it clear that the pain and suffering does not grow less. The hidden underside of all Péguy's mysteries is itself the mystery of pain. He would have understood Theodore Roethke's lines:

> Is pain a promise? I was schooled in pain,
> And found out all I could of all desire;
> I weep for what I'm like when I'm alone
> In the deep centre of the voice and fire.
> I know the motion of the deepest stone.
> Each one's himself, yet each ones everyone.

Péguy was such a man. In the depths he cried out his own *de profundis,* in the heights his own *Te Deum,* and both were infinitely rich. But their quality was nowhere more truly disclosed, more humanly expressed, more spiritually charged, than in the moments of *approfondissement* that he used to attend to what fatherhood meant to him. He returned to it again and again, passing steadily from one level of perception to others. Who knew anxiety like the father of a sick child? Who gave hostages to fortune like the father of a family? Who hoped that his life's work might bear fruit like a father working for his children?

In all his pictures of that relationship Péguy sketched out the lines of something which he believed to be at the heart of the creation and therefore at the heart of prayer. No poet perhaps since the gospels were first written has put more weight upon two words, 'My Son'. Few men can have believed more intensely that a man might pray for ever and not exhaust their wealth. 'The meaning of a word lies in its future use' even though when we use it now its meaning is present with us. Péguy was always hearing ahead, always exclaiming with wonder at that which was now and yet to be disclosed. In the words 'My Son' the heart of the Divine Father was made known to mankind. His children had been launched upon a cruel and turbulent sea, in their fears and weakness they would behave most cruelly and foolishly to each other, in their pride and ignorance they would forget even Him who gave them their life. Yet:

Ask a father if his best moment
Is not when his sons begin to love him like men,
Him as a man,
Freely,
Gratuitously,
Ask a father whose children are growing up.

And so He waited for them and gave His own Son for their
sake. They would, because of the divine engagement of the eternal and temporal, in time grow up and inherit all that He had
planned for them. In the meanwhile they were there to be watched over, to be loved and tended, and always to be played with.

Coda

A man dreamed.

His eyes were open but he was in darkness. He was dismayed and troubled by it. This darkness enveloped the world and seeped into his own soul. He knew himself to be assailed by darkness; its horror clutched at him, weakening all sense of purpose, yet he stood upright and felt constrained to move.

Before him the ground appeared to rise, a hill that he must struggle to climb, though why he had come there he did not know. Even in the darkness the ground seemed strangely familiar to him. He had no fear that he might lose his way. He had a sense that he had been there before among crowds of people. He had been much moved by what he had seen and shared in. He had a feeling now that they had all gone away deliberately. Defection charged the darkness, giving him still more the sense of being alone. He felt turned towards a greater loneliness than he had ever known before. Yet he pressed forward, upward, stumbling and gasping at times for breath. He reached what seemed to him to be the summit of the hill, the struggle to climb was less intense, and suddenly he stopped.

In front of him, barely discernible in the darkness but real enough stood a shaft of wood set in the earth. Somewhere above his head as he strained to see he believed there was a crosspiece too. He did not touch it, for with a feeling of revulsion he knew quite well what it was. The cross in the darkness seemed to make heavier his sense of being alone. It had been used no doubt as crosses were, but now even the body was gone, taken away and buried, and this deserted hill was left to him alone. What was it that had brought him there? What was there he could do? What was there that anyone could do?

Now that the darkness had come to enshroud the hill, could any man do more than simply wait till it cleared away? Wait in the hope that it would do so? It struck him suddenly as strange that never until now had he been so utterly hopeful that the daylight would return. He was puzzled by his own discovery until he began to realise that there was nothing else in his mind but hope. All else had gone. All the things that he fancied that he remembered as he came up the hill had quite unaccountably but surely slipped away into the darkness. He did not even wish to go after them to try to find them now. The space that they had filled, the attention that he had given them, was what he now needed for this hope, for nothing else now mattered but this hope. What he hoped for he could not tell. 'When the light returns', he thought, 'I shall see things as they are', and this left him oddly satisfied in the darkness that enveloped him.

For some time, it seemed, he stood there uncertainly before the cross whose outlines were if anything clearer now. And then he started suddenly as if seeing something else. He closed his eyes, opened them, and looked again. He saw now, this was certain, behind the cross another shape. It was a tree, a living tree set in the ground. Its bole and sprawling roots he could just make out. Somewhere above him in the darkness he realised there were branches and moving leaves. The gardener in him came to life; he felt some kinship, some affection for the tree, and he put out his hands towards it.

At that moment strange things happened. Without warning of its approach, a violent wind blew suddenly all around him, blew so vehemently that he found it difficult to stand, yet stand upon his feet he felt he must. The wind roared in his ears and pushed and beat upon him from every side. The darkness seemed now like waves that reared themselves against him. He struggled to keep his feet upon the ground, to stay upright before the tree. He was conscious now of the sound of the wind in the branches of the tree, of the struggle of every leaf to retain its place. He had seen trees stripped and shrivelled by the wind, he had seen them smashed and broken to pieces. But he was confident now, with a curious sense of elation, that this tree could withstand the wind.

This tree had grown up among such winds, battled against them and prevailed. There was no need to be afraid for it. His confidence in it seemed to unite him with the tree. He was grateful for its strength.

It was the cross that troubled him. The wind already seemed about to break it up, and yet in a quite inexplicable fashion he felt that this must not be allowed to happen. He was there to see to it that it did not happen. As he strained to see it again it cracked and shivered beneath the wind. A slight flapping noise above his head made him peer upwards to where he could just make out a scrap of paper that fluttered, nailed, it would seem, to the cross but now being blown to shreds. Well, the paper could go; what was left of it now could hardly matter, and these notices put up in public places were so little informative of things that most men wanted to know. He'd read them sometimes and been none the wiser, and now, it was too dark to read what remained of it. Very soon the wind would finish it off. What words had been there would by now have been blown about the world, and perhaps when daylight returned some pieces would be picked up and read. 'To those whom it may concern' . . . if indeed there were any. It was the cross that needed his attention. He must save the cross. As the wind howled and wrestled with him, it came into his mind that he could do so if he tied the cross to the tree. They were not too far apart, if only he could find some rope.

How utterly foolish it was to suppose that anything of the kind would be lying about in the darkness of that lonely hill, but crowds had been there and crowds left litter. He began to search. Dropping upon his knees he felt round in all directions. It was marvellous, even revolting, what there was to touch on the dark ground. Grass and stones, bits of metal, a few coins, fragments of food, now and then some thorns and a nail that pricked his fingers and made him wince. It seemed a fruitless foolish thing to be doing. But then, there it was, a piece of rope, then a strip of leather, slipped off and discarded maybe when the prisoners no longer needed to be bound, thrown down and trampled on, but now exactly what he needed.

Back at the foot of the cross he slipped the rope round its shaft and bound it to the tree, surprised that the rope was long enough, and confident now that the wind could not destroy his work. For a moment he remembered binding up slips of trees that he had once grafted with some care. It was a job that called for some skill and he was pleased that he could do it. But even as he thought of it the foolishness of it swept over him. He was binding the dead wood of the cross to the trunk of a living tree. How men would have laughed to see him doing such a thing down there in the orchards where he worked. What fruit, they would have jeered at him, do you expect from grafting of that kind?

But now he felt too tired to face his folly. The wind still roared and beat upon him, still tugged at and rocked the tree. The darkness hung over him as thick as ever. He had done what he could. He put out his hands now to steady himself against the cross.

And suddenly he slept. How long he slept he did not know, but even before he opened his eyes he knew that the wind had dropped and the darkness had gone. He felt glad and unafraid. When he opened his eyes and looked up he saw that the cross was intact, saw the nail where the paper had hung before it was torn and whirled away. The cross was saved.

Then he stared again. The rope was knotted about it. He had done his job well. He was pleased. But where was the tree?

The light enfolded him, he knew he was not alone.

Bibliography

1. Texts
Péguy. *Oeuvres Poétiques.* I volume.
   Oeuvres en Prose. 2 volumes.
   Bibliothéque de la Pléiade. Gallimard. Paris.

2. Translations
Péguy. *The Mystery of the Charity of Joan of Arc,* translated by Julian Green,
   Hollis and Carter. 1950
Péguy. *The Holy Innocents and Other Poems,* translated by Pansy Pakenham,
   Harvill Press, 1956
Péguy. *Temporal and Eternal,* translated by Alexander Dru, Harvill Press, 1958

3. Biography and Comment.
Dru, Alexander. *Péguy.* The Harvill Press, 1956.
Halévy, Daniel. *Péguy and Les Cahiers de la Quinzaine.* Dennis Dobson, London, 1956
Villiers, Marjorie, *Charles Péguy.* Collins 1965

4. Books referred to in the text.
Adams, H. *Mont St. Michel and Chartres.* Constable, 1913
Alves, Rubem. *The Theology of Human Hope.* Anthony Clarke, 1975
Arnold, Matthew. *Collected Poems,* Oxford, 1909
   Essays in Criticism. MacMillan, 1927
Assman, H. *Practical Theology of Liberation.* Search Press, 1975
Bloch, Ernst. *A Philosophy of the Future.* Herder, 1970
   Man on His Own. Herder, 1970
Brenan, Gerald. *St. John of the Cross.* Cambridge, 1973
Bronowski, Jacob. *The Ascent of Man.* B.B.C, London, 1973
Buber, Martin. *Between Man and Man.* Kegan Paul, 1947
   The Knowledge of Man. Allen and Unwin, 1965
Burckhardt, Jacob. *Reflections on History.* Allen and Unwin, 1943
Chadwick, Owen. *The Secularization of the European Mind in the 19th century.*
   Cambridge University Press, 1975
Coleridge, Samuel. *Biographia Literaria.* Dent (Everyman ed.)

Daniélou, Jean. *Prayer as a Political Problem.* Burns & Oates, 1967
Dansette, A. *Religious History of Modern France.* Nelson, 1961
Day-Lewis, C. *The Room and Other Poems.* Cape, 1965
Eliot, T.S. *Ash Wednesday.* Faber, 1930
   Little Gidding. Faber, 1942
   The Sacred Wood. Methuen, 1920
Frankl, Viktor. *The Will to Meaning.* Souvenir Press, 1969
Gardner, Helen. *Religion and Literature.* Faber, 1971
Goldman, L. *The Hidden God.* Routledge & Kegan Paul, 1964
Green, Julian. *Diaries.* Harvill Press, 1964
Gregor-Smith, Ronald. *The New Man.* S.C.M, 1956
Heidegger, M. *Being and Time.* Blackwell, 1967
Heschel, A. *Who is Man?* Oxford University Press, 1966
Hügel, F. von. *The Mystical Element in Religion.* James Clarke, 1961
James, W. *Varieties of Religious Experience.* Longmans, Green, 1923
John of the Cross, St. *Complete Works.* ed. E. Allison Peers, Anthony Clarke, 1974
Johnson, Martin. *Art and Scientific Thought.* Faber, 1944
Jones, David. *Anathemata.* Faber, 1972
   Epoch and Artist. Faber, 1959
Kierkegaard, Søren. *For Self-Examination.* Oxford University Press, 1941
Larkin, Philip. *The Less Deceived.* Marvell Press, 1958
Lawrence, D.H. *Lady Chatterley's Lover.* Penguin ed. 1951
MacMurray, John. *Persons in Relation.* Faber, 1961
Muir, Edwin. *Selected Poems.* Faber, 1969
Murdoch, Iris. *The Sovereignty of Good.* Routledge & Kegan Paul, 1970
Nédoncelle, M. *The Nature and Use of Prayer.* Burns and Oates, 1964
Pascal. Blaise. *Pensées.* Everyman ed. (Dent)
Pfleger, Karl. *Wrestlers with Christ.* Sheed and Ward, 1936
Pound, Ezra. *Cantos.* Faber, 1957
Powys, J.C. *In spite Of.* Village Press, 1974
Powys, T.F. *Mr Weston's Good Wine.* Chatto and Windus, 1928
Roethke, Theodore. *Collected Poems.* Cape, 1954
Rutherford, Mark. *Autobiography.* T. Fisher Unwin, 1900
Sales, François de. *Introduction to the Devout Life.* Burns and Oates, 1937
Speaight, Robert. *Georges Bernanos.* Harvill Press, 1973
Steiner, George. *After Babel.* Oxford University Press, 1975
   Language and Silence. Pelican, 1969
Thoreau, Henry. *Walden,* Everyman ed. (Dent)
Weil, Simone. *Gravity and Grace.* Routledge and Kegan Paul, 1965
Zaehner. R. *Concordant Discord.* Oxford, 1970